The
SECRETS
of LIFE

Also by Stuart Wilde

Books

Affirmations
The Force
*God's Gladiators**
Infinite Self: 33 Steps to Reclaiming Your Inner Power
"Life Was Never Meant to Be a Struggle"
The Little Money Bible
Miracles
The Quickening
Silent Power
Simply Wilde (with Leon Nacson)
Sixth Sense
The Three Keys to Self-Empowerment
The Trick to Money Is Having Some!
Weight Loss for the Mind
Whispering Winds of Change
*Wilde Unplugged: A Dictionary of Life**

Audio Programs

The Art of Meditation
The Force (audio book)
Happiness Is Your Destiny
Intuition
"Life Was Never Meant to Be a Struggle" (audio book)
The Little Money Bible (audio book)
Loving Relationships
Miracles (audio book)
Silent Power (audio book)

*Not published by Hay House

Please visit Hay House USA: **www.hayhouse.com**®
Hay House Australia: **www.hayhouse.com.au**
Hay House UK: **www.hayhouse.co.uk**
Hay House South Africa: **orders@psdprom.co.za**
Hay House India: **www.hayhouseindia.co.in**

The
SECRETS
of LIFE

STUART WILDE

HAY HOUSE, INC.
Carlsbad, California
London • Sydney • Johannesburg
Vancouver • Hong Kong • New Delhi

Published and distributed in the United States by: Hay House, Inc.:
www.hayhouse.com • **Published and distributed in Australia by:**
Hay House Australia Pty. Ltd.: www.hayhouse.com.au • **Published
and distributed in the United Kingdom by:** Hay House UK, Ltd.:
www.hayhouse.co.uk • **Published and distributed in the Republic
of South Africa by:** Hay House SA (Pty), Ltd.: orders@psdprom.
co.za • **Distributed in Canada by:** Raincoast: www.raincoast.
com • **Published in India by:** Hay House Publishers India: www.
hayhouseindia.co.in

Editorial supervision: Jill Kramer • *Design:* Tricia Breidenthal

Library of Congress Control Number: 2005935719

ISBN 13: 978-1-4019-0736-5
ISBN 10: 1-4019-0736-9

10 09 08 07   5 4 3 2
1st edition, November 2006
2nd edition, January 2007

Printed in the United States of America

---

*I dedicate this book to all
those fringe-dwellers who had
the courage to make a run for it.*

Dear Friends,

This is a new and revised edition of a successful book I wrote awhile back. These thoughts and ideas form the basis of a philosophy that allows for a liberated mind-set and a more carefree and delightful life.

The quotes are from my books and my unpublished writings. In addition, I've included excerpts from TV and radio shows that I've done over the years, and from newspaper interviews or articles that I've written.

Open the book anyplace and start reading. Usually you'll find that whatever page you happen upon will contain helpful hints on some aspect of your life that's currently on your mind. Somehow, the synchronicity of life always leads you to what it is you need to know. So if you're like me and you want your spiritual concepts "short and sweet," then this book will suit you perfectly.

When you think about it, life doesn't have to be complicated, so if you stay balanced, develop perception, become detached, concentrate on what's real, act powerfully, and believe in yourself, there's not much else you'll ever need. And that should be the primary objective of your selected path in life: spirituality, emotional freedom, and liberation.

Sincerely,

Stuart Wilde

On Powerful Thinking

Be brave, think like a warrior, and live like a monk. Don't eat like a bird. A bird eats twice its own body weight each day.

On Seeing Beauty

The way to motivate you to a new perception is to try to see the beauty in all things. There's beauty even in ugliness. Anyone can look at a rose and call it beautiful, but try seeing the beauty in a friend who's deliberately ripping you off—that's harder. Go for the beauty in every little thing; it will carry you toward a new destination.

On Love

Love is a settled heart and a big heart. Love encompasses everything inside of you.

On Femininity and Spirituality

Femininity is the key to spirituality. Unfortunately, I'm male, but I was born surrounded by women, and that might have helped. I have a twin sister who was born with me. I think I must have learned things. The grace of God is feminine. What else does one need to remember?

On Daydreaming

Daydreaming is very important to your mental health. It's particularly useful in your chosen profession.

On Softness

Spirituality is soft. To be soft you have to let your guard down and agree to be a bit vulnerable. There's spiritual warmth in vulnerability, and there's a coldness in being hard. Soft wins in the end . . . hard is swept away.

On Hiding
Your Spirituality

Spirituality is quite a mysterious thing—keep it that way. If people can see your spirituality, you've degraded it.

On Silent Power

One of my most successful books is *Silent Power.* Power that is obvious, which people can see, often manipulates others through obedience and fear, but silent power is a spiritual power—a heightened perception that doesn't have to be manipulative. It's like a light or a grace you express that you use to assist you on your path through life.

On Eccentricity

In a world where everything and everyone is required to be the same, eccentricity and individuality will get you banned from almost everywhere. I've always felt that it's better to wander off in one's madness than to sit in shackles with the others on the bus.

On Democracy
for the Enlightened

Unfortunately, there's no such thing as democracy for the enlightened. With a system based on one person/one vote, you're bound to have a social order designed to pander to the survival fears and tribal psychosis of the masses. By becoming somewhat enlightened, you'll always be slightly odd, a bit of a weirdo, because you've gone beyond the petty issues of the collective mind-set. You have to accept that you'll never fit anymore. You become a "fringe-dweller." Don't fight it—there are millions of us.

On Fringe-Dwellers

There are millions of people who are fringe-dwellers—that is, they don't fit in. They're not terrorists or subversives; they just silently believe in alternative things. It's as if they're here on Earth, but they have one foot in a higher dimension. I love the fringe-dwellers because they offer us hope.

On Knowing Things

It's not what we know; it's what we *think* we know that becomes dangerous. It's a wise person who insists on nothing in particular. It's okay to have an opinion, but it's foolish to insist on it. There's so much we don't understand about life and this universe; we're all bound to be proven wrong in the end.

On the American Camelot

A former teacher told me that Camelot was in fact a transdimensional world superimposed on this one, a hidden dimension inside this 3-D earth plane. He told me about an American Camelot that appeared mysteriously in a valley in Nebraska in the 1850s. He said that it was called Findley.

A stagecoach got lost in a storm, and it stumbled there by accident. When people walked into Findley, they disappeared. When the occupants of the stagecoach eventually came out of the valley, many years had passed even though they thought they'd only been gone for a few weeks. Findley existed for 12 years, then the transdimensional overlay withdrew from that valley, and everyone who lived there walked out into the real world once more.

I once wrote a movie script about Findley, but it never went anywhere. My script is in another dimension—the attic!

On Fat Time

Have you ever stumbled into a time warp whereby time seems to stand still? I call it "fat time." One day there were eight of us in a Mongolian yurt in a field in England. I talked for a few minutes, told a very short story, and then we all came out of the yurt. We thought that we'd been in the tent for ten minutes or so; we were shocked to discover that almost four hours had passed. Where the missing time went we never discovered.

The next day a pal visiting from America also went into the same tent. He lost three hours as well. Time warps have an eerie wonderfulness to them.

On the Out-of-Body Experience (OBE)

Decades ago, I did a seminar with the out-of-body guru Robert Monroe. The OBE process didn't work for me right away. But six weeks later I had a spontaneous OBE while I was at work at the office. It has only happened to me once, and on that occasion I never got out of the room. I just hovered up by the ceiling, then after a short while I twanged back into my body.

The OBE is interesting, but you can have fascinating inner journeys without struggling to leave the body. Once in New Orleans in the summer of 2000, I spontaneously went through a wall. I was gone for almost an hour, although it seemed like just a few minutes to me. I don't know what force took me through the wall, but whatever it was, it brought me back round-trip. Nice.

On Mirror-Worlds

There's a mirror-world to this one. We each have an alter ego, a doppelganger of us that's evolving in there. It looks exactly the way we look.

Our walking intellect is here on Earth, and while our subconscious mind, our inner impulses, are here in our minds, they also exist in another dimension, the mirror-world.

So, it's important to clean up what we really feel about people and the world in general, as those feelings make up our "real" selves, the spirit identity that's simultaneously in the mirror-world—the one we'll meet when we pass over.

On the Afterlife

I discovered a great secret: Once your brain ceases to function, there's no mechanism for remembering you or your life. A life that cannot be remembered would be a waste of time. People say that we have an eternal soul, but what is the mechanism of its memory? What is its source of power? An eternal soul would have to have an eternal power source, and where does that power come from, and what is the mechanism of its memory?

Then in the trance state I saw the mirror-world, and I saw how our subconscious identity is in there acting out our feelings in an alter ego, while we're still alive here in this world. So I realized that the waking intellect drives information-gathering for the subconscious mind, and that the subconscious exists in two places: here, and in a mirror-world dimension that's just yards away from us at 90 degrees.

Continued on next page

The intellect ceases at death. It can't operate without a brain. It's the subconscious and its identity in the mirror-world that acts as the perpetual memory of you. It's your soul and your identity in the afterlife.

The secret is that you're in the afterlife now, while still alive. That means you're in the spirit world while here on Earth, and you can still fix your mirror-world, spiritual identity if it's a bit dark and dubious.

I came to see the mirror-world using a phenomenon I call the Morph. I haven't discovered the eternal power source of the mirror-world.

On the Morph

The Morph is a transdimensional phenomenon that transforms the ambience of a room. It's very common now—it's everywhere, and thousands of people around the globe have seen it. When the Morph descends into a room, it looks like dry rain or swirling mist. There are vortexes in it, and fast-moving striations of energy, and we also see little sparkles in it that I call the "specked ambience." The Morph makes the walls and floor of the room go nonsolid and soapy looking.

I first saw the Morph with 15 other people in March 2001. The Morph takes oxygen out of the air so it never descends all the way down on top of you. If you're on a bed watching the Morph, it's always a couple of feet above your head. When you put your hand up into it, your fingers start to morph dramatically to the right from the middle knuckle. It looks very odd, and after a while

Continued on next page

your hand and even your arm dematerializes. The room has to be quite dark for you to see this. You can see the Morph in bright light, but you have to be very sensitive.

I've found that the Morph acts as an optical lens, and through it you can see into other worlds, which is how I found the mirror-world and the information about the afterlife. I've lain on a bed every day, sometimes 20 hours a day for three and a half years, watching the Morph. That is how I found out about the spiritual dimension, which is as close as 90 degrees to us.

Facing north, stretch out your left arm and point to the west. The mirror-world is about three feet off the end of your fingers. Heaven is much closer than we originally realized!

On
Transdimensional
Travel

We often wait for the light at the end of the tunnel. It was the tunnel at the end of light that made me nervous.

On *The Matrix*

I've seen the film *The Matrix* 57 times. I found it fascinating, as much of the story is true in the inner worlds of the Morph and the mirror-world. The real matrix looks like a honeycomb, and there are doorways in it, tears that weren't there years before. Also, those green Japanese-style tumbling letters are very real. I see them in the Morph all the time.

The Matrix tells how the persecution and subjugation of humanity by superhuman dark forces is broken, and how people are eventually set free. I think the descent of the Morph is how that stranglehold will be broken.

On Proper Gratitude

To redeem yourself, you have to enter the darkness of your shadow-self and understand it. Ingratitude is part of the modern "Gimme, gimme" society. We're raised to expect things for free.

Here's an important perception: The first step in healing your soul from its hidden darkness is to develop proper gratitude. Gratitude is a resonant chord deep from your heart that says you're truly grateful for every small mercy. All other types of gratitude are platitude.

On Separateness

Separateness is the religion of a false god. We are all brothers and sisters here.

On Loneliness

Loneliness is a karma people suffer when they make their mind too important. By separating from nature and humanity, the mind goes dark and cold; it's the lack of heat that makes you lonely. The cure is easy, but you have to agree to step out and embrace people, life, animals, and the magnificence of all things.

On People

One of the things I like about humanity is that there's lots of it. It would be a hell of a drag if you had to wander around for days just to find someone to talk to. Try talking to strangers if you don't already do so. Be warm, listen to them carefully, and care for them and their needs.

On Transition

One day I'm going to a place where animals, children, and all of their toys talk to each other, and they invent games to play that no one has ever seen before.

On the Third Presence

For 20 years I silently strived to establish the *Third Presence*. There is good and there is evil, and the <u>Third Presence</u> is *deliverance*. I'll let you know if I delivered on deliverance about ten years from now.

On the Human Shadow

Accept and honor your shadow. If not, it will come and nibble your toes at night when you least expect it. Redemption comes from understanding your shadow-self and processing it into something more reasonable and more spiritual.

On Redemption

People say that redemption comes from following the rules of one religion or another. While that might be so for some, I discovered something interesting in the inner worlds, in that redemption has very much to do with heat. Warmth eventually grants you absolution. It's the warmth of your heart and your kindness to others that redeems you in the end. Elitism is cold, and it separates you from others, and over a long period of time it creates sentiments inside you that carry you toward a hellish state of being.

In the mirror-worlds, hell is cold and heaven is pleasantly warm. I found that very intriguing.

On Deliverance

Thirty years ago, my ol' teacher said that at the end, initiates would appear on Earth to lead people to safety and that these initiates would show people how to walk into another dimension. He pointed out that it was as easy as crossing a room while removing your overcoat.

When he said these things, I was fascinated, but a part of me wondered if it was real or if it was all just hocus-pocus. Then in 2001, I started to see visions of very tall beings who could run quite fast. Some were female, but most were male, so I called them *Tall Boys*.

I recently saw five Tall Boys in real life, not in a vision. They were standing by a fire in a beautiful garden at the edge of a rain forest. They were enormous, 12 to 15 feet high. What was fascinating was that where they stood there seemed to be a hole in reality, as if they were inside a cardboard cutout with a dotted line around them. I felt that if you wanted to walk out of here, you would walk through the center of one of the Tall Boys. It was as if their very being acted as the frame of a transdimensional doorway. These are fascinating times.

On Elation

Elation is a good habit to embrace!

On the Collective Unconscious

What I have seen of the collective unconscious led me to believe it wasn't worth collecting.

On Turning Points

One day a few years ago, I got fed up with being me. That was a big turning point.

On Dedication

It's rare that you meet a person who's truly dedicated. When you do, you'll find that he or she almost always has a delightful energy and is usually successful.

Dedication is the warrior's prayer unto him- or herself. It's a mode of fierce concentration, in which you become so attached and devoted to your cause that eventually life has to give you everything you desire. Dedication is vital. You have to live your life like the warrior-sage, with spirituality in one hand and a sense of purpose in the other.

On Perseverance

You have to be ready to take advantage of situations when they arise. Perseverance allows you to hold on while the energy of the Universal Law delivers.

On Challenging Yourself

Just getting through life isn't enough. If you have any kind of real goals, you'll want to challenge yourself as well. People find a little rut to follow and they stick to it. This is because the mind doesn't like spontaneity or change. People tend to create patterns that they're comfortable with, and they pursue that path day in and day out. Everything is fine for 20 years, then one day there's a bear on the path and it eats them. Tut, tut.

On the Sacredness of Things

The things you believe in often form the baggage you carry with you in this life. The wise person isn't usually dogmatic; he or she is content to believe in the sacredness of all things, living in the spontaneity of energy, trying not to defend or judge too much.

The mind of the sage is eternal and infinite. In seeing beauty in all things, he or she accepts the ways of man, including restriction and strife. Without constraints there would be no spiritual growth for any of us.

On the Memories of Trees

I met a shaman in Ireland who talked about the memories of trees. He said that trees retain a memory of the humans and animals that have passed by, and that the trees take on certain characteristics. He took me to a "healing tree," and then to a special hawthorn, which he said was a place for people to sort out their psychiatric problems. There was another place in the woods where people had spontaneous out-of-body experiences and so forth.

I went to the woods with the wily Celt many times. I saw lines of energy, usually golden in color, sometimes lime green, about a foot off the ground. When you cross one of those lines, it trips the memories that the trees hold. Nature is symmetrical, and humans are

Continued on next page

often asymmetrical; we are bent out of shape because of our emotions. The forest tries to restore the lost balance within us as we pass.

One day there was a young lad with us. He was nice enough, but he was rather tricky and very cocksure of himself. He became very scared and sick, and he kept insisting that we should interrupt the walk and take him to a hospital. The shaman had seen his type of antics many times before, so he ignored him. But still the lad insisted. Eventually the shaman grabbed him forcefully by the lapels, shook him, and said, "This forest is the hospital, the only hospital we have."

I learned a great lesson that day. I trust the woods and the trees now. In the past I didn't understand or know about their memories and their powers.

On Shamans

There are hokey shamans and real ones. The real ones can enter into your body via the etheric and the mirror-world and heal you. The fake ones just bang a drum, and nothing much else happens.

On the Kogi's Aluna

The mystical Kogi people of northern Colombia call the mirror-world the *aluna*. They take special children at birth and raise them in a dark cave for nine years, where they're not allowed to see the outside world. In this way, the children come to see the aluna naturally, and then after nine years have passed, they leave the cave and enter the physical world. These mystical children grow to become the shamans and the wise people of the tribe. These shaman-leaders of the Kogi people are called *mamas*.

I met a seven-year-old child-shaman who wasn't a Kogi, but his father had been with them for two years. The boy had extraordinary powers. Sometimes I'd see him in the mirror-world giving advice, and other times he'd be taking action of one kind or another. When you see people who are still alive on Earth, taking action in the aluna, it means that they have a special power.

The child wore ceremonial white robes decorated by beads, and around his neck was a thong with a jaguar's tooth on it. One night there were

35 of us around a fire, when the boy rose at about midnight and started telling us a hysterically funny story about a circus and a piece of bread that could talk. His story lasted an hour or so. It was beyond funny.

Then I saw the child-shaman in the aluna (mirror-world). He was sitting down in his white robes, and he placed nine mushrooms in the air in a circle all around himself. The mushrooms had long stems, and they hung in the air as if by magic. Then he looked at me as if to say, "Are you watching?" I nodded, and then he spun the mushrooms slowly around and around himself as if they were planets in orbit. The mushrooms made three or four complete revolutions of his body, and he then turned to me and smiled. I nodded again, also smiling, and then he and the mushrooms disappeared like a soap bubble bursting.

In the Bible, Jesus said, "Suffer the little children to come unto me." I don't think we have to suffer them. They are already there.

On "Where the Hell Am I?"

If you think about it, none of us is actually here on Earth, for we are not our bodies or our minds. Rather we are a Higher Self, a spirit identity in a body. This body is a space suit from which we peer out at a strange world. But the "real you" has never landed.

Yet in bouncing about on the earth's surface, we tend to forget that the space suit (the human body) is not the real us. Meanwhile, there's a Higher Self in the other world beaming us guidance on how to keep the space suit in one piece and how to get the most out of our "Earth walk." The overall control mechanism of our comprehension is beyond Earth. Life is just an experiment to see how well we can listen and cope. It's all a matter of gathering experiences for other spiritual adventures coming later.

On Dimensions

Spirit is subtle. It doesn't bang you on the head with a plank. It allows gradual growth as you discover a deeper and deeper meaning to the world around you. Dimensions are inward; they unfold to energy like those Russian dolls that you take apart to find another doll inside, and yet another, and so on. The only thing that bars you from experiencing those infinite inner spaces is incompatibility between your energy and the dimension you wish to experience.

More on Dimensions

In the transdimensional worlds, it shows our Universe as being very small; a galaxy would fit in the palm of your hand. It also shows that each human is a new universe in the making, meaning that a star system out in space is also an evolving being. We are incubating our souls inside a universe that is also a spiritually evolving being. Our fast human life is an evolution of 70 or 80 years; we have to stretch our minds to imagine a universe-style being that has an evolution of a hundred billion years, say.

Dimensions scramble your mind. Now this may fry your noodle, but some of the most powerful spiritual beings in the nearby dimensions are insects. If that idea bugs ya—well, tee-hee. I'm not sure what to tell you other than imagine an ant that can carry 100 times its own weight. We humans are weak in comparison.

On the God-Force

The God-Force is a light, crammed full of information that is digital and fractal in nature, as are all things in the universe. The light is always moving toward you. It's like a divine wind blowing in your direction. Religions call it different things, but it's just a power. It's more than intuition; it's an inner knowing that grows because you understand its infinity, and you recognize that the power is within you and connected to all things. That's beautiful. It will teach you hour by hour, day by day.

The reason it teaches you is because the force is information, and at this point you're moving beyond Earth experiences, so you've got to have something to help you or you'd flounder. But you'll never be able to touch it, taste it, smell it, or see it, but it's with you at this very minute.

Continued on next page

As you begin to trust this power, it will lead you step by step. It knows who you are and what you need. How does it know? It knows because it's all-knowing and powerful, so it seeks the same for every part of itself, and you are one of those parts. It will take you to the next person; it will take you to the next place. It knows what parts of you need work in order to become stronger. If you work on those parts and change those aspects, then suddenly a door opens. There's a whole new dimension waiting for you, but it doesn't want you coming in with any old stuff. Once you're rid of the stuff, in you come.

On Disciplines
Before Dawn

Through silence and the power of nature, you revitalize the inner you. Predawn is your strongest hour. If you can rise in time to meet the day, that effort becomes a prayer, a discipline that you use for establishing control over your mind.

Its power comes from the fact that at that time people are usually asleep, and there's very little psychic pollution to hinder you. Use the time to project yourself mentally into the day. As you center your mind, your power goes out and surrounds the people and events that you'll meet, acting as a spiritual forerunner and enlivening the energy in front of you.

By setting up your day before the rest of the world has risen, you establish an energy that cannot be overwhelmed by the negativity of others.

On Waking in Love

Some mornings I wake up in love with everybody and everything. It's most distracting; I can't get anything done. The trick to loving people is going past the discomfort you feel about yourself and the circumstances of your life.

On Avoiding Confrontation

One key to establishing control over your mind is to spend a part of each day completely alone, even if it's only for ten minutes. Use the time to review your feelings and concerns—allow an emotional maturity to develop whereby you understand that this is a dream and nothing is real.

The old Taoist sages understood the importance of maintaining control and avoiding confrontation. They taught that life is like a stick floating down a river, and that interpersonal strife snags it, bringing your progress to a halt. Confrontation fuels the ego and strengthens the power of the fake you over your affairs. The sage walks away; the fool stands and fights.

On Seeing
Things as Perfect

We cannot go beyond the Earth plane while criticizing its faults, for they serve us, as all restriction does. To transcend beyond this plane, you first have to be able to accept it as is, and see beauty within it, no matter what. You have to see it as perfect in its imperfection. Then you develop the spiritual maturity to leave things as they are, understanding that there's a greater knowing here that seeks balance, and it knows what it's doing.

On Surrender

I used to shake my fist at the injustice of the world, and I'd rile against tyranny. It made me sad and weak, and it robbed me of energy. In the end, I saw that the key to everything is to surrender. I can fix myself but not much else. Surrender offers us the hope of victory in the end, but we have to wait.

On Flowers

There are no words to describe the exceptional beauty of a flower glistening in the morning dew. Have you ever stared into a flower for ten minutes or so? After a while you begin to see universes in its center. It seems to me that each flower gives off a tone. It isn't audible in the normal sense, but if you're very still, you can hear it in your mind. It seems to me that the spirits that exist in the flowers must be very pure. I must say that if I were very small, that's where I'd go for a rest and a little nap.

On Gaiety

There's a gaiety to life, a carefree beauty, and as you begin to develop a philosophy of life that's carefree, you become a wonderful scamp whose heart is light and whose soul is brightly colored. Our world needs gaiety; it has been ruined by politicians, lawyers, and serious people.

On the Lushness of Life

They say that the lush things of life make you fat. And they're probably right. But if you constantly deny yourself the lush and sensual things of life, eventually your spirit gets too thin. It's better that you're a little overweight and that your heart is full and rich with life's experiences than winding up with a thin body and an anorexic spirit.

On Animals

Personally, I've never met an animal I didn't like. I can't say the same for all the humans I've met. When I look into a dog's eyes, I see the spark of God in there, and that spark is saying to me, "Stu, try to be as honorable and natural and pure as this dog, for I, the God-Force, am inside this animal, and it is in Me. And when I set the evolution of this world into being, I, the God-Force, had to think of an unobtrusive way of watching what is going on. I chose the animal kingdom, for it is humble and honorable, and it is through the eyes of animals that I watch and evaluate the progress or lack of progress that humans attain."

On Insects

People don't usually like bugs and insects, but without them we'd be in a sorry mess; they're vital to the balance of our ecology. Here's something surprising: In the inner fractal worlds that are the basis of our universe, there are insects that are more evolved than we are, and they act as our healers. I know that it sounds daft, but it's true. Imagine a praying mantis six feet high that can perform intricate brain surgery. It's very hard to comprehend. We think we're at the top of the pile, but we're far from it.

On Dancing

I know that dancing is nothing more than organized wobbling, but not having a lot of natural rhythm in my bones, the pleasure I experience in dancing is more than wiped out by the silliness I feel as I try to get things to wiggle coherently. But I'm willing to keep trying. My twin sister is a very famous dancer, and that inhibited me a bit.

On Understanding the Sacrosanct Nature of Your Life

This lifetime is yours, just yours. You may be involved in relationships and love others, but basically what you make of your life and how you pass through it is your evolution. That is why adversity is useful.

In desperation, we begin to pull on our unlimited power; and we realize that anything can be changed, that suffering is a product of the inner self, and, by looking at our inner selves, we can transform ourselves. To overcome something once and for all means going within to discover the real causes of the disturbance.

This process of discovery will allow you to have more energy, which you can use to create the things you want in your life.

On the Nature of Beliefs

In daily life, your feelings, thoughts, and attitudes are your metaphysical order form. So before you decide to change your present conditions, you'll have to be sure of what you want from life. The currency with which you're going to pay for it is belief. To create something with absolute certainty, you have to establish the feeling within you that it has already been granted—that the condition you desire is already a part of your life.

On Assessing Your Plans

Ask yourself prior to committing to anything, "Do I have the wherewithal to pull it off, and do I know what I'm getting into?" What is your motivation for taking action? What is the level of your commitment, and do you actually want the end result or are you going for something else instead? Are you trying to capture a castle you don't really need or want?

On Concentration

Concentration is an important discipline in personal growth and development. Ernest Holmes said that your power goes where your consciousness flows. When you're centered and concentrating on what you're doing, not only do you derive more pleasure from your actions, but also all of your power, both inner and outer, is being used to empower those actions. Through concentration you become powerful. Force your mind to concentrate and you've won a battle over struggle.

On Being
Very Important

"Hello, God, remember me? . . .
Oh, well. Never mind."

On Relationships

Get out of any situation that endorses negativity, causing you imbalance. People come together in relationships for growth, not for life. If a relationship sustains you, that is, if you're both growing from it, and if it's beautiful and it has energy, you're together for good. If not, either fix it or ditch it. You don't need situations that don't support you or that lower your energy. You don't owe anything to anyone.

The only real responsibility you have is to work on yourself to raise your energy. That will become your gift to the world. Pull back from negative situations and negative people. You don't need to judge them or try to change them. Just allow them to follow their path. You may want to give them a little shove, but if they won't move, you move. Never mind security; preserve your soul.

On Staying Awake

Often we're so busy "doing" life that we forget to experience it. We end up missing most of it, so try to notice everything all the time. By doing so, you'll wake up to your perceptions and develop a sixth sense. You can see around corners with a sixth sense.

On the Nature of the Quest

If somebody suggests something to you that seems terribly easy, quite often the mind will like the idea because you know you're good at it. But sometimes the easy things aren't your best choice. By testing yourself in your weaker areas, you challenge yourself and become stronger. A path that tests your ability can still have a lot of light.

On Golden
Opportunity

If you move toward your goals, expressing all your power, opportunity will find you as a result of your actions. For by riding your energy and knowing and believing that your Higher Self is with you, you'll be in the right place at the right time. But make the first move, taking constant care to purify and review your life; move from negative habits into a fortress of light. Discipline is the horse you ride on.

On Going Beyond
the Current Situation

As you do your job immaculately, your energy will stand out like a neon light because almost everyone else is doing a rather lousy job. Wherever you find yourself right now, do a fantastic job. By doing so, you'll eventually go beyond it. Bit by bit you energize yourself into various different positions until you get to where you really want to be. The light that's guiding you will always show you the next step. It's always there at every stage of the journey. Feel it out, but don't think too much.

On Overthinking

If you're wondering . . . don't wonder. Overthinking is a trap. It's a bad habit, one that you should get out of. There usually isn't an explanation for much of what happens. If we knew all the reasons why things happened in life, we'd be wise, but we'd also be very scared. There are many things we're not supposed to know, so it's better that way.

On Walking Slowly

The trick in life is to walk, don't run. Go into every situation with calmness, appraising it in the light of your expertise. Doing so allows you more freedom. You pull from a reservoir of strength that's very different from the way most people live life. It sets you apart and grants you mystery. People wonder why your life seems so effortless compared to theirs.

By nurturing mystery and developing your ways in secret, people grant you a reputation that's actually greater than that which you've achieved so far. It helps you. It's "outer hype," which isn't hype you've created yourself, but hype that others have created for you. It can be very useful, especially when you're wondering what to charge.

On Staying Calm

Over many decades I learned to be very calm when faced with danger. When my mother-in-law walks in, I instantly go into a catatonic trance.

On Clarity and Clutter

Decide what's important to you: your home, your family, your job—whatever. Then gradually eliminate those things that are superfluous. By doing so, you become ever more clear as to what you actually want. That's important, for if your life is very cluttered, you usually won't know what you want, so the energy of life reflects back to you with uncertainty.

If you genuinely don't know what you want, begin by eliminating those things that you know you don't want! In simplifying your life, you become stronger. But first you have to bag the clutter.

On Healing the Planet

The healing of the planet will take place once individuals feel comfortable accepting their reality, wherever it might take them, with the understanding that life is, in effect, a heroic journey of self-realization, not just a quest for self-aggrandizement.

Once this thought-form correction takes place, the world will automatically heal itself; and humans will truly experience a golden age of creativity, love, and personal fulfillment.

On Competition and Energy

If you're a spiritual person, you don't need to be involved in competition. Instead, be involved in energy. Once you get into raising your energy, there is basically no more competition. You're out there on your own in the marketplace of life, and you can more or less do what you like. You'll find that people will be drawn to you.

On Acceptance

To come to a full and permanent acceptance of evolution allows you to enter into a purity of spirit that's not normally attained by others. It's the final resignation, whereby you settle into an acceptance of who you are; and you rest in the reality of what you are, rather than in the fantasy of what you are not.

Your acceptance of life is an outpouring of your inner sense of spiritual awareness rather than a by-product of fortunate circumstances. The secret is to concentrate on changing yourself gradually, as fast as your inner self can accept that change.

On Metaphysical Strength

The more powerful you are, the more ability you have to materialize your wants. One's metaphysical strength is like a bank balance. It represents the time lag between what you conceive for your life in your mind and when it actually appears. Weak people imagine forever and nothing much shows up. For the less wimpy variety, their thoughts show up in various forms, but it's less than they'd hoped for. In the strong ones, events show up more or less immediately. The sage can materialize the burning bush in the flick of a thought-form; most others would have difficulty materializing a box of matches over six months.

On the Real You

The real you, the inner you, is pure, very pure. It is loving and magnanimous. It understands. It has patience. It is tolerant—it will wait forever while your ego trots about trying to figure life out. It's pleasing to remember that back home there's a friend who's waiting for you to stop being silly, who's waiting to welcome you with open arms if and when you show up.

On Operating Immaculately

I've never been good at understanding the immaculate, but a pal of mine who's a very successful writer talks about it all the time. He suffers from all the usual "gringo" diseases: pornography, brothels, drugs, self-importance, denial, and so on. I think his "immaculate" is something to do with not getting caught.

I try to tell the truth to myself all the time, and I try to stay away from extreme materialism and the gringo diseases. At best we can only do what we can, and try not to create any more darkness in the world. I feel that I'm a million miles away from immaculate, but I wonder if those who speak of the immaculate life aren't hiding stuff. Tricky, eh?

On Expanding Yourself

Most people think that raising your energy means meditating and eating stewed veggies. All that stuff helps, but there are other ways you can raise your energy fast. Go out and buy experiences for yourself. Do new things that challenge you. Force yourself to go and meet new people. Meeting people is vital. Sooner or later you'll need a hand up from where you find yourself, and someone has to give you that helping hand. The more *some-ones* you know, the better chance you have of making it to the promised land.

On Abundance

I want you to expect that things are going to sustain you. Why shouldn't they? Life sustains itself. Get used to beginning to work with your feelings so that they express a powerful energy, a feeling of abundance. That feeling of abundance has nothing to do with how much money you've got. Abundance is saying, "I feel rich in my feelings. I feel rich in the friendships where I have love to offer. I have a good mind."

Feel abundant in nature, in the naturalness of all things. Feel strong, and never mind if you don't have much money right now. Create energy and feel abundant—that's the secret to turning things around.

On Quest and Money

I believe that we're all on a metaphysical quest. You may not necessarily describe your life in those terms, but I believe that we're here to understand ourselves; and that includes the physical plane, which encompasses the body, mentality, emotions, sexuality, motherhood, fatherhood, and cash. You simply must have cash; otherwise, the tail wags the dog. The trick to money is having some. There really isn't anything else to it. It amazes me how many people miss that point.

On Not Quantifying Things Too Much

Once you accept life without struggling against it, you can see that everything serves you in one way or another. A lousy meal helps you appreciate and remember a good meal. A defeat strengthens you for the next victory. If you try not to quantify and judge things and accept them as part of your overall experience, you become mature. All of a sudden that power that should have been yours from the beginning is returned to you as a calm individuality—a creative stillness that allows you to *be*. Acceptance unshackles you from the restraints that you've created for yourself, and it allows you to explore inside your own individuality.

On Overcoming Restriction

If your feelings are closed down and narrow, you eventually pull many forms of restriction into your life because what you're putting out is restriction. Restriction and control are endemic to all of our societies. It's taught in school. Everywhere you go in the Western world, you see nothing but control and restriction of the people. It's amazing. But people are used to it. They like it.

It's as if somebody comes along and thumps you on the foot every hour with a mallet. The first time you'd be annoyed, really annoyed. But by the second hour, you'd be a little less angry. Once the person had been thumping you on the foot every hour, on the hour, for ten years, you'd actually be sitting there waiting for him, thinking, *Oh, he'll be along in a minute,* because you'd get used to it. You'd think, *Oh, he's late; what happened to him?*

That's how we are. It's difficult unless you stand back and look at the situation, to conceptualize the level of restriction that you accept into your life. By opening your heart, you're affirming that you're prepared to break out.

On Developing an Alternative Philosophy

If you want an evolution that's different from the tick-tock, everyday rhythm of the masses, you're going to have to develop a philosophy that's diametrically opposed to what the other folks believe. If you're in the consciousness of the masses, you're bound to wind up in the destiny of the masses. You won't want that—trust me on that one. People are on their last legs, tottering like drunks in the street on New Year's Eve.

On Practicality and Flow

There's a very subtle balance between being in the flow and trusting that the God-Force will bring you all the things you need, and doing things that will ensure you get what you want. Once you understand that, you can say, "I'm in the flow, I trust in the beauty of my own inner light, but I'm also doing these 35 very practical things to make sure I don't get my rear end mangled." Be practical, and try for a mangle-free life.

On Stepping Beyond

My ol' teacher used to say that four times in a person's life, he or she is offered the chance to step spiritually and metaphysically beyond the confines of the physical plane. Very few accept the offer, for it means that you have to control the mind and the negativity of your life, and discipline yourself to enter into a more spacious reality.

At first the transition is like crossing a fast-moving stream—it's tricky. You have to watch your step, but it's not too hard. If you refuse to take the first step the next time you have a chance, it will feel like crossing a raging river. If again you refuse, the power of your mind and your ego grows and grows, and making that transition will feel like swimming in a very large lake with all the effort and consistency that entails. Finally, the battle for supremacy of your life will take immense strength, and it will feel like you have to swim across a great ocean. The name of the game is to bite the bullet, taking your chances early when they're offered.

On Not Letting People Tow You by the Nose

As you get more and more independent and more powerful, and the less you succumb to tick-tock and embrace your own philosophy and alternative ideas, you're not going to care so much what people think about you. You didn't come down to the Earth plane to keep the other six billion people happy.

Try this quirky discipline: For the next 30 days, don't do anything for anyone without charging for it. When you're asked to give someone a lift to the station, tell them it will cost $10. If they ask why, tell them, "This week I feel good about myself. This week I'm learning to empower myself, so $10, please." And when they argue, make it $20. When you feel okay about charging people, then you can do things for nothing and play the nice guy, for you know that you can include yourself if and when you have to. That's important. Otherwise the world tows you around by the nose.

On Loving the Self

Consciously and subconsciously, we're constantly trying to get people to love us. But in pushing for love and acceptance, we're often saying that we don't like ourselves very much. We hope for someone to make us okay and right.

If you love yourself—not in an egotistical sense, but in the sense that you're just silently satisfied with who you are—you know that you aren't perfect and you'll work on it bit by bit, and that is good.

Once you feel more comfortable with yourself, people find it easier to accept you. When you feel insecure about yourself, other people pick up on it and they react. Your insecurity rattles their insecurity fears. When you're strong, they feel safer.

On Femininity

Females have a fantastic advantage over males, in that they have a natural spirituality. They don't fall for the same power trips.

On Female Support

If the female will subjugate her ego and support the male unequivocally, the male goes beyond his identity crisis and begins to understand himself. The energy he projects will then become stronger. He pulls in more money, and the family gradually does better. But it's difficult for the female to subjugate her ego, for often the male is weak and that causes her anxiety. She quite rightly feels the need to control. But there's a balance between being cold and mean and the more spiritual approach. If she can do it, it will work really well. If she can't, there are other ways.

On Kindness

At the end of your life, you will be judged not on what you did or how many children you raised or what you managed to subjugate and conquer. The last judgment is all about kindness. If you were very kind to humans and animals, it shows that you had a warm heart. If you were cold and cruel to others, you slide toward a spirit world that's cold and cruel.

On Avoiding
Indecision

Seventy percent of all the people I've surveyed in my seminars don't know what they want. If you *do* not know what you want, you're putting out indecision and mixed messages into the energy of life. Circumstances tend to reflect that indecision back to you, saying, "Listen, mate, if you haven't got a clue, we haven't got a clue either."

Get focused. Decide what you want and life will deliver it to you. Perhaps you have everything you need for now, which is why you don't know what you want.

On the Benefits of Restriction

Restriction can at times be good for you, for it binds you into circumstances so that you're forced to work on yourself. It's sort of an insurance policy that makes sure you don't get too far out ahead of yourself until you're absolutely ready. But once you grow metaphysically, the restrictions around you no longer serve you. That's when you need to bag it and flee.

On Fear

It's okay to be scared from time to time. Sometimes just taking responsibility for your life may feel scary. Fear forces you to stay awake. The point where you "click" from living in your mind to trusting the inner you is a major turning point for many. It's how they gradually transcend fear.

If your mind dominates, you'll become scared; but if you feel things out instead, most of the fear falls away and you know deep within that it will all be okay in the end.

On Teaching Children to Stay Safe

What I used to do is take my little lad and a few of his mates out in the street and show them how to read people. You mentally reach out and grab a molecule of another person's heart as they pass you. It's subtle, because it's all in the etheric realm, but if you practice it a bit, you'll soon get it. I'd ask the lads to tell me about passersby. They soon understood which ones were scary and which were to be trusted.

I'd tell the kids to watch for "Kung Po" eyes. People who are psychotic often have a white space between their irises and their lower eyelid. Charles Manson the mass murderer has Kung Po eyes.

On Feet

If somebody is imposing on you in a way that you don't like, then move. Feet are a wonderful gift. Animals are lucky in that they have more feet than we do.

On Living
the Lucid Dream

When you're driving to work and there's a guy in front of you doing 15 miles per hour and you're honkin' and getting angry and you're saying, "This idiot, why is he going so slowly?" then relax. Realize that he's going that speed because that's how far he wants to push the little pedal. He's got all day to make it down to Safeway and back. He doesn't understand that you're 30 minutes late for work. We all have to live in each other's lucid dream.

On Philosophies

Who said that understanding life is hard? The greatest concepts are the simplest. If somebody brings you a philosophy on a cart with books piled high and says, "Here, join this," then run. If they bring you a philosophy that's written on a few little itty-bitty pieces of paper that say, "The pub opens at 6 P.M.," ask, "How do I join?"

Less is best. Short philosophies are light and breezy. You need light and breezy in this life.

On the More You Know, the Less You Know

We think that spiritual understanding has to be a big complication. By making it complicated, we seek to make it more grand and more real.

But in reality, you don't have to be clever to be spiritual. In fact, the less bright you are, the less trouble you'll have. Because the more clever you are, the more of an intellectual approach you will come out of, and the more you have to negotiate the labyrinth of your mind to get to the light. You can just intuit it—there it is, *plop,* like an omelette falling off a plate. Easy.

On Weakness

Don't worry; you'll grow spiritually in spite of any weaknesses you may have. That's the way human evolution is organized, and a good thing, too, for most of us.

On Guilt

Once we humans moved from a spiritual relationship with God to an emotional, survival-based relationship with Him, then we developed sin.

Once we had sin, there was only one way we could go: backward. Because even if you're doing everything right 99 times out of 100, on the 100th occasion when you forgot to fling the scarecrows off the cliff, you're in trouble. You feel worthless. "Oh my God, the tribe didn't go through the ritual this week." What do you feel when you feel guilty? You feel worthless.

Once we had sin, we were given guilt, then we developed worthlessness.

On Going Beyond the Earth Plane

When you move in your mind beyond the day-to-day consciousness of the Earth plane, you never tell 'em you've gone. It's easier and safer that way.

On Walking Away

There's a point in your spiritual evolution where you may have to walk away from the old system; otherwise, you're constantly being jangled by the dichotomy of who you really are as an infinite being, and what you have to pretend to be in order to fit in. The more infinite you become in your spirituality, the more difficulty you'll have adapting to a very restrictive, manipulated society.

On Society's Rules

Rules suck, in my philosophy, anyway. I like to be pope in my own church. "Our Stuie who art in Heaven, hallowed be My name. My kingdom come, My will be done . . ." It may sound a bit egocentric, but it's an original excuse for avoiding most of the rules.

On Joyousness

In theory, joy should be a natural part of our lives. Somehow that isn't always true. We get so caught up in the crazy, frenetic pace of modern living that we get disconnected from the inner part of ourselves that naturally rests in a state of equilibrium, at peace and at one with all things. As such, we almost have to make joy a habit, a long-lost friend to see. In the craziness of life, we shouldn't lose sight of the beauty, the calm, and the purpose to things.

On "It Ain't That Serious"

You know when you watch people rushing around? It seems like they're taking life incredibly seriously. They're often hurtling about making everything mega-important. And yet when you think about it, their seriousness is really a sign of immaturity. It's a sign that says: "I don't feel safe, and I don't feel that I control my life, so I'm going to create an incredible ballyhoo around me and everybody else just to make sure we all make it."

And yet, seriousness is so childish because life really isn't that serious. When we can back off, we see that one result or another doesn't really make that much difference in the long run. And yet, seriousness always comes out of an egocentric sense of weakness. So if you're surrounded by a bunch of people who are incredibly serious, what I suggest you do is this: Get a lemon meringue pie and walk into your boss's office and smash it in his face. And say to him, "Oh, you silly old twit, just back off. What about a little fun in life?"

On Personal Freedom

The whole function of the evolution of humans on the physical plane as I see it (in what are basically extremely restricted circumstances), is to eventually become free. If you don't win your freedom, you spend the entirety of your life in prison. There are prisons of our physical bodies that won't clunk along. There's emotional restriction where you find yourself trapped by circumstances, or the confinement created by the society or the family you're from. Or you have to endure restriction because you have no cash and everybody's telling you where to go and what to do.

The way to tackle the problem is to select one or two areas that you know you can fix without much effort. Untangling those knots gives you the space to build your power so that you can tackle the harder stuff. Eventually you break out of all the things that bind you.

On Law and Freedom

Is a minute of democracy every four years personal freedom? I wonder. When you look at the statute books, there are more than a million laws there. If you began to read them today, you'd be six feet under before you ever got to the end. There's a law for everything—legislative diarrhea by control trippers.

There's a crossing-the-street law, a walking-the-dog law, millions of parking regulations, tax laws by the ton, and there's a law for every single move you make. What can you do? We're chickens in a coop.

I dropped out and became a perpetual traveler. You only incur a tax liability if you live in a country for more than six months. That helped me detach from the oppression of it all, and that sense of injustice. The secret, I suppose, is to detach.

So, if somebody says to you, "What do you think of government?" your reply should be, "I try not to." In that way, you can get on with your life without being emotionally sucked into everything that's going on. Personal freedom is partly a state of mind.

On Accountants

It's called crunching the numbers 'cause the numbers make ya numb! I like my numbers in a paper bag—cash flow that you don't bother to count.

On the Police State

In a police state, you have two options: join the police or emigrate.

On Freedom and Democracy

I was watching a bit of "freedom and democracy" on the telly. It looked awfully violent and dangerous to me. I'm not sure how much more freedom and democracy we can take before there's no one left in the world.

On Being in the Flow

I believe that life was never really meant to be a struggle, but somehow we're taught that life is one of effort, hard work, anguish, difficulty, and battling on, regardless. Yet, when we look at nature and we look at what's around us, we see simplicity and flow. Does the tiger get up in the morning and say, "I'm gonna try hard today; I'm gonna jog around the block and stick alfalfa sprouts up my nose and eat my vitamins, and I'm gonna really struggle like crazy and hopefully by lunchtime I'll get something to eat"? No, it doesn't.

It just gets up, has a little sniff under its tiger armpits, wanders out into the forest, and there on the path is lunch. It's the same for you if you get into the flow and you pull away from the emotion of struggling. Sure, you may have to drive across town to pick up a check and take it to your bank, but it doesn't have to be anguish—it doesn't have to be laced with emotion. Effort is part of the physical condition. Struggle is effort laced with emotion. And you don't need that.

On Poverty

At times, poverty is helpful because it allows you to understand wealth. After you've done poverty for a bit, you wake up one morning and think, *Sheesh, I've had enough of this.* It motivates you to trot off and make some dough.

On Partying

If you're not in bed by midnight . . . come home.

On Weak Marriages

The trick to marriage is pickin' a good one, because if you're going to commit yourself to somebody for the rest of your life, why would you want to hitch up to somebody who's weak and ineffectual? It's a recipe for an uphill climb. What's the thrill in owning four bricks in the suburbs with someone you can barely tolerate?

Stay single until a good one comes along. That's the best way.

On Soul Mates

The secret for a male is to temper his outgoing sexuality, and to cultivate inner softness . . . understanding that there's strength in softness. For a female, the key is to accept her position as custodian of the spiritual, inner energy of the world, for she has a natural spirituality within her.

Then, if a spiritual male and a spiritual female come together as soul mates, they can create a powerhouse of light. The challenge is to pull to yourself the spiritual person you need to create the missing link. You don't need a slug for a soul mate. Many of you have tried that; it didn't work.

On Love and Marriage

Just because you fall in love with somebody is absolutely no reason to marry. If you put out "Send me anyone," then you'll usually wind up in a relationship that you don't want.

On Disease

Disease is scary, but it's also beautiful. It serves a good purpose because if you run your body like a train through the night, where the driver is in the restroom and the whole bloody thing is hurtling down the hill at 90, then what happens is, the body jumps the track. At that point you realize that you've got to get the driver out of the restroom and back up to the front of the train. Disease is handy—it stops you from killing yourself.

On Teachers

People say that as a teacher you should be perfect and set a good example, but that's nuts. If you're perfect, you don't need to learn anything; and if you don't need to learn anything, you wouldn't be a teacher.

On Maintaining Your Philosophy

If people say, "I think your philosophy is the pits," you can say, "Well, thank you, I appreciate you sharing your opinion." Then if they say, "I think that what you believe is stupid and you're dumb and you're not righteous and you're not gonna get to heaven and you're gonna have a lousy time," you can say, "Thank you for your opinion—it helps me concentrate. I particularly liked the way that cockroach walked around your coffee cup while you were talking about my life. And what threw me into a state of absolute ecstasy was when the cockroach stopped, looked up at me, winked, and then urinated in your coffee. I loved it. I totally loved it."

On Honor

The way people look at honor and a love for their country can make you wonder. They use it to get sane. The theory is that right-minded, honorable people go off to some dusty road in the Middle East and get their bloody liver blown off. And when the guy's sitting there with his liver 45 yards away, people say, "Well, how do ya feel?" "Honorable, man. I feel real honorable—I'm doin' it for king and country."

Now, I'm not saying that all of those guys are wrong, for they feel a need, but it seems to me that there must be an easier way to be honorable and show love for your country.

On Nobility

My father was a noble man. He was an officer in the British navy. Seven times he was singled out for bravery in action during World War II. He told me that it's more important to be noble and brave than it is to be rich. I got it in the end, but it took me a while.

On Limitlessness

Once you realize that you're not your body and you're not your mind and you're not your emotions or the fate of the nation you were born into or the color of your skin or the religion that you believe in, but that you're the divine spark within . . . then you become limitless. And that is the key to mysticism; that is the key to understanding life.

On Declaring Yourself In

Everything is out there waiting for you. All you have to do is walk up and declare yourself in. No need for permission. You just need the courage to say, "Include me in." If you say it with conviction, no one challenges you and no one realizes that this is your first day on the job and that you haven't got a clue which way's up. If you act as if you've been in the game a thousand years, no one will guess differently.

On Truth

Truth is my friend.

On the Way Things Are

The way things are is the way things are. Accept that. By doing so, it sets you free. Then if you don't like the way things are, you can set about changing them. But the first point of your empowerment over circumstances is to stop struggling against them and accept them.

On Understanding

There are many things that I don't understand. I like it that way. It took me a long time to realize that having to know the answer to everything is a trap. There are loads of things to which there are no real answers—not yet anyway. So if your mate Harry ploughs through the front of the 7-Eleven, you can sit and wonder all day why that happened, or you can just accept that it did. Sure, there's a reason for things, but what good will it do to trouble yourself over them? Maybe Harry needed to be out of the Earth plane in a hurry. They're not called "convenience" stores for nothing!

On the Drama of Evolutionary Experiences

When you read about some horrific disaster, or whatever it is that the media is trying to feed you this week, you're concerning yourself with something that isn't your reality. It has nothing to do with your evolution. You need to detach from what's going on and look at it from an infinite viewpoint rather than the more finite survival issues that dominate people's lives.

On one level, maybe 300 people hit a mountain in a plane that wasn't flying quite high enough; but on another level, everyone's infinite, so none of them is dead. They all exist in a spirit-world dimension. Then you can avoid the emotion and say, "Interesting evolutionary experience."

On Scare Tactics

The media operating on behalf of the government loves to offer us a perpetual drip, drip, of scary stuff. It's a form of control, but it's also a way of lording it over us. They have the scoop on the latest threat; and they're graciously letting us know, offering advice, warning us, blah-diddy-blah.

You need that rubbish like a hole in the head. In a hundred years or so, our current leaders will be seen as some of the most evil people who ever lived. Stay calm and see the propaganda game for what it is. They're just trying to wind you up.

On Struggle

To justify the fact that their lives are out of control, strugglers like to feel that struggle is noble—that somehow God is testing them. If you were God, you might shed a tear over that one. The God-Force doesn't ask us to struggle, nor does it ask us to endure pain. All of these are conditions that humans have imposed upon themselves, for it's easier to do nothing and struggle than it is to bring forth a creativity from within and work hard to deliver it to others.

On Life

Ask yourself, "Am I having a good time, right now?" Having a good time is Job #1. Sometimes we forget that.

On Manipulation

If a person says, "I am a master" or "I am the initiate," you can tell from the very fact that they're saying it that they are not it. If you were a master or an initiate, you wouldn't have to tell anyone. Usually what these characters are doing is manipulating people into becoming followers. That's cash flow, not spiritual growth.

Don't elevate others to a divine status; it will mess with your mind, and sooner or later you'll begin to believe it. If anyone tries to kiss your foot, stand on their hand.

On Freedom

If you're not totally free, then ask yourself why not. It's sad to abdicate control of your life; and if you did abdicate, did you do so voluntarily, or have you allowed someone to force it upon you? Maybe insecurity or greed trapped you, maybe laziness trapped you, or maybe a lack of courage trapped you. Your soul is beautiful. It needs to breathe.

On Shopping

Shopping is marvelous, but try to shop in nice places. Only the rich can "afford" to go shopping in bargain stores such as Wal-Mart or JCPenney or the like. If you aren't rich, you'll never become so by shopping in those places. Go uptown and buy less . . . but buy good things of high quality.

On Good Eating

If you're going to be in tune with the energy of life, you'll be living on life-sustaining, natural foods. If you see an ingredient written on the back of a can or a packet of food that you don't understand, then you know it can't be very good for you. The life force has easy words, like *carrot*.

On Vegetarianism

It is sad to kill things.

On Detachment

Learn to detach. Emotion rots your soul. You forget how to think properly.

On Being Peaceful

You don't want to mess with world peace—all you need to do is be peaceful. If you get caught up in the struggle for world peace, it will stir you up and create anger and hopelessness. The world will be peaceful when people grow up and get off their macho trips, which isn't anytime soon.

On Simplicity

Once you've taken on metaphysics and you see yourself as infinite and have developed some kind of creative money-making endeavor outside of tick-tock, then the final goal is to return to a simple lifestyle, whereby the outer game (keeping it together and paying the rent) is so unassuming that it doesn't impinge on or disturb your inner spirit. Having made all these changes in your life, and having taken on new activities and a new way of looking at things, eventually you have to return to a purity of spirit, a simplicity in which you become nothing.

On Identity

When you can stand up and say to yourself, "I am the God-Force, I am God, and It is me," the first step of you reunification is complete.

On Leaving
Things Alone

If a tree in the forest isn't perfect, you don't go up to it and say, "Excuse me, tree, but I don't really like the way you look. Would you mind if I lop a bit off?" You just let it be. You respect it and leave it alone.

Look at people as if they were trees. If they ask for advice, give it. If they don't ask, walk on.

On Life's Reflection

What you're looking at as you peer out through your eyes is a reflection of you. It is all constantly you. There's nothing that you see that isn't you. As you watch the outside, you're constantly watching a reflection of the inside. It's teaching you about yourself. If the cab driver slows down to pick you up and he sees you standing there in the rain and he gives you the middle finger and accelerates, that's your energy that's pissed him off. He's felt your energy and voted no. If you cause reactions, start to look at why people are reacting. Often it's because you're trying to control them.

On Death

A famous author who writes books about conspiracies told me that he and his wife aren't going to die. He said that they're just going to walk out of this dimension into another one. He's a bit eccentric, but I liked his idea even if it isn't true in the end.

The fact is that we've all bought into this thing about dying. But you may say, "Everybody dies." How do you know that everybody dies? Because if a person doesn't die, how would you know he didn't die? The guy who didn't die would be living beyond you. So you aren't going to be around to find out whether he died or didn't die.

Death is like a club we join. The agreement frightens you. The fact is, we agreed to it. My ol' teacher said that there are people here on Earth who are over 1,000 years old. He said that they're humans who have moved from a physical body to an etheric one, but they never left; they stayed to help. Interesting, eh?

On Dematerialization

A Colombian shaman I met showed some of us how to walk in and out of the mirror-world *aluna* using the hallucinogenic brew ayahuasca to help us perceive it. It was amazing information. I've been watching the mirror-world via the Morph for almost five years, but I didn't know one could actually walk into it.

When you walk in, you disappear momentarily. Late one night I was watching an American man, an astrologer, smoke a cigarette by a fire in a garden. He had this mirror-world aluna thing worked out as he dematerialized four times. Three times he was gone for about a minute or so, but on the last occasion he was out of sight for about ten minutes. His cigarette stayed in this 3-D reality, so I knew where he was on the lawn by watching his glowing cigarette floating mysteriously in midair. It was so much fun; it really played to that part of me that's like a little boy.

The mirror-world aluna is the place of the scattered Camelots that I've been promising in my writing for a long time. I'm happy now, as I know how the dream will come about. People will dematerialize and walk in there.

On Just Being

The fruit tree doesn't jump out of the orchard and knock on a supermarket's door and say, "Hey, do you need any of these?" And you, too, should not try and force yourself on others. Let them know you exist and what it is that you do, but wait for people to come to you. It's stronger that way. The less you appear to need people or their business, the stronger the power, and eventually the greater your success.

On Trust

To allow yourself to be moved metaphysically, you have to know and trust that all is well. To strengthen that trust within you, begin to move away from the concerns of the people. You must begin to believe that all is well with the world: that there is a long-term plan even if you don't necessarily understand it.

But more important than knowing and trusting that all is well with the world, you have to know and trust that all is well with you. You have to be satisfied with yourself. Because if you're dissatisfied with who you are, and because you exist in an eternal inner self, you're at this very moment eternally pissed off. That's not much of an affirmation. It's like an itch you can't scratch. It will distract you from the main thrust of your desire, which is to grow spiritually.

On Disengaging
from the World

Nothing is good or bad, cold or hot. Nothing is long or short—long in relation to what? You could walk five miles in the pouring rain and say, "This is a long journey." But is it a long journey compared to walking across the Sahara? When you disengage from the world, you judge less, and when you pull away from quantifying the world around you, you understand a great secret.

You'll understand that you can just experience it all as a feeling rather than as a decision or as a quantifiable something or other. Your life is an experience. It's not a high-or-low, failure-or-success type thing. It's just an experience. When you treat it as an experience, you come out from the ego and the mind into a more infinite perception and you don't try to figure it all out—you just concentrate on living.

Do you understand that when you don't say, "I like it" or "I dislike it," that it allows you to have a more infinite experience of whatever it is that you're considering? When you don't quantify the experience, it expands eternally, and you become freer in your perceptions. And what happens if you don't quantify your life? It lies there in all its spiritual purity, limitless.

On Coming and Going

I think that the secret to good sex is to make sure the male doesn't finish too soon so that the female can move through to a point of orgasm. Most guys can be done in about two seconds flat—in the space of one Coca-Cola commercial, so if they're not doing their best to hang in there, the whole thing's over and done with. It can be rather disappointing for the girl.

On Male Sexuality

You read in the Taoist texts that males lose power or chi by ejaculating. So in the olden days, the monks would put jade rings on their thingies to exert control and to become, theoretically, immortal. I can understand that if you ejaculate too much, you'll tire yourself out, but I can't understand the philosophy of never ejaculating at all—that's nuts.

What's the point of becoming immortal and having a crummy time getting there? It's like having a Ferrari in the garage and walking everywhere. Seems a bit stupid to me.

On Kundalini and Immortality

As a young man, I read all those Taoist and Hindu texts that show you how to raise the sexual kundalini from the root chakra to the crown and become immortal. I spent a number of happy years pondering it all. Then it suddenly struck me that if there's one thing that all those Taoists and Hindu immortals had in common . . . they're all extremely dead.

Oh, well, you win a few, you lose a few.

On Beginning Things

You can only begin where you find yourself. It sounds so simple, but most never get started because they're waiting for just the right circumstances or the right person to help them get going. Might be a long wait.

On Time

How much time have you got? All the time in the world, I'd say. Why? Because you're infinite. Remember that. Don't let life put you on the "hurry up." Repeat it three times: *I have all the time in the world. I have all the time in the world. I have all the time in the world.* You'll soon get it.

On the Power of Now

Ram Dass wrote *Be Here Now,* and Eckhart Tolle wrote the bestseller *The Power of Now.* Now those were good ideas. These guys got it right, in my view. There isn't any necessity to constantly project your mind into the future; it disempowers the present. If you're putting on a picnic three Saturdays from now, you may have to do some organizational stuff today to make sure that it happens. But that isn't projecting your energy forward. It's saying, "In order for us to have a picnic three Saturdays from now, we need to order some picnic baskets today."

The idea is to develop yourself clearly inside the present and not pollute the future with too much thinking so that the place where you are not (the future) is clear and open and ready for you to arrive. That helps you strengthen the present. People are sometimes poorly defined because they're confused. Their energy is everywhere other than in the here-and-now. In polluting what is not yet real, they debilitate what *is* real.

On Where Things Are Not

The Taoists taught me something valuable. They showed me how to look at all of what a thing is and also at what it is not. In some situations, what is not there is often as important as what is there. A tree is defined by its leaves and branches; but it is also defined by the sky around it (where it is not), so the sky defines its boundary.

Then when you look at your life, you can see what is real, what is here right now, and you can also think about what is not here right now. That helps you identify who you are, and it helps you become real. It allows you to strengthen yourself by living in the truth.

On Opposites

In metaphysics, we look at the antithesis of things: the opposite. And as you begin to look at things more and more from a metaphysical viewpoint, you see the opposite as being a vital part of the whole. The antithesis is as important as what is.

On the Antithesis of Things

There's an antithesis in life that actually complements what you are, and you can use it. It's like the shadow in the light. You can't have light without a darkness in which it will shine. So you have to honor the darkness that assists the light in becoming something. That's why I don't have much time for those woolly-headed characters who say that the world ought to be all cozy and lovely and guaranteed.

The Utopian lovefest isn't going to happen, for if it did, all the human spirits evolving through the Earth plane would suddenly head off. There would be no challenge. We would all return to the spirit world where the lovefest is a lot better. You can't have courage unless there's weakness. You can't have goodness unless there's a notion of evil. And you can't have spiritual growth unless there's something for you to knock up against. You should thank God that things aren't perfect.

On "Don't Let the Suckers Grind You Down"

You've always got to call everybody's bluff. Ninety-nine times out of a hundred, call their bluff and you'll get away with it. If they try to maneuver you, call 'em. When they say, "If you don't do this and that you're gonna be outta this job," answer, "Fine. Here's the key to the executive restroom—eat it."

If you always call their bluff, nobody can maneuver you because you're strong. Why? Because you're not coming out of lack or fear, like this is the only job in the world. You're not coming out of survival, or there isn't enough to go around. You're not coming out of "there's a rush." You've got all the time in the world. All possibilities are open to you. Don't let people manipulate you by trying to play on survival issues. Stay on the high ground. Don't let the suckers grind you down.

On Calling
Your Own Bluff

As I've said, you've got to call everybody's bluff. And when you really get strong and secure, you've got to call your own. In becoming acutely aware of your own BS and lies and exaggerations, you move toward becoming a truly spiritual person.

On Negotiating

I know that the win-win philosophy in negotiating is very popular nowadays. And there's nothing wrong with that. But are you really here to keep everybody happy? Most of you have been doing that for far too long. You're here to master life and to make it simple and quick for yourself. So when someone asks, "How much do you want?" you reply, "All of it." It's a great place to start, isn't it?

If they say, "What about win-win?" you say, "Here's the deal. Under the laws of win-win, you'd be happy with 50 percent, right? Okay, let's do this: You take 25 percent less than what you want, and I'll take 25 percent less than I want. That's win-win. We'll both reduce our expectations by 25 percent."

A lot of you have gotten out there: bright-eyed and bushy-tailed, you put it all together, but you forgot to ask for what you wanted, or you devalued what you wanted. The name of the game is to ask for what you want. Start with "all of it," and work back from there. It's a good exercise in assertiveness.

On Your
Word as Law

The words you use are very important; you are the general, and your mind is your foot soldier. It believes whatever you tell it. If you say, "This is hard," the mind accepts that, and it creates the "hard" circumstances to fit the opinion you've given it. If you say, "It's simple," that's how it will be. You decide. Your words are much more powerful than you might realize. If you moan that life's a pain in the butt, you'll wake up with hemorrhoids.

On Nurturing Yourself

Our lives are designed to sustain the edifice of things. The more stuff you have to sustain, the more complicated your life becomes. Then life is no longer designed around your pleasure, your energy, or your nurturing. Instead, it's a welfare office that you use to sustain the desires of others. What's the point of that? You have to nurture yourself and take care of your needs first.

On the Government's Largesse

If the government makes a mistake, you get to pay for it. If there's a disaster, you pay for it. If the politicians decide to send $3 billion to some obscure place in order to win the local vote back home, you get to pay for their largesse. All this can get on your nerves.

But once you realize that the system of power isn't designed to nurture or benefit you, you can concentrate on working on yourself and develop a consciousness outside the evolution of tick-tock; and at that point you don't give a damn who's getting the money and who isn't. You just incorporate enough bigness and abundance in your soul to include all the bizarre things the government is going to bill you for.

On Flaky Governments

All of the governments have let all of the people down, all of the time. That's history. Once you understand that, you can stop wondering what the hell they're going to do next and get on with your life.

On State-Sponsored Violence

State-sponsored violence is always couched in a heroic poeticism. We bomb people to "liberate" them; we assassinate people in the cause of national security. Our attackers are called peacemakers; their defenders are called terrorists. Our dead soldiers are heroes; their dead soldiers are just the nameless dead. Stay away from heroic poeticism; it will rot your soul if you align with its sentiments.

On Pride

Pride that you express to other people is probably ego. Pride that you express silently to yourself is real pride. Pride of self is understanding that life is glorious, and that it's an honor to be here. Appreciate what you are, and accept that.

On Femininity

It's important that the female develop a reality that honors and nurtures her femininity and that she develop an identity and creativity of her own. It's equally important for the male in the relationship to endorse that creativity.

On Feminine Softness

What makes a woman beautiful is the softness she exudes. It isn't a physical beauty. It's an inner softness, the warmth, the purity, the caring, and the nurturing. It's not the shape of her body or the shape of her face. Many women who have beautiful faces have revolting energy.

On Masculine Power

Males understand power by doing things that are powerful. Women just understand power.

On Fighting Evil

Some years ago I mounted my high horse of indignation and went out to fight evil: human evil, transdimensional evil, demonic ghouls, black magicians—anything satanic, I'd plow in. I scored some fantastic successes, and I suffered many more defeats. And I took endless etheric hits, thousands of them. In the end, I got tired and sick, and I nearly died a few times along the way. Eventually I had fought to a standstill. I didn't lose and I didn't win. There was always more evil.

So I got off my high horse, and I realized that fighting evil is stupid. I took to a new idea that I call "cheesy denial." You smile and pretend that everything is just fine. But in the end, cheesy denial becomes painful because it endorses lots of lies. So I tried isolation for three and a half years as a cure for cheesy denial, but I got lonely. So now I'm twiddling my fingers waiting for a new formula. I think it's called surrender.

On Throwing Chickens to the Crocodiles

Sometimes we're obliged to placate ugly people who are above us—at work, for example. Throwing chickens to the crocodiles is a way of saying that at times we have to massage people's egos or butter them up, or we have to pander to their illusion of specialness. Sometimes we're forced to make gifts and concessions so as not to bring further mayhem upon ourselves.

It's pointless to resist—just lob chickens as fast as the reptiles will eat them. Then flee.

On the Linden Points

There are two points on either side of your spine that are vulnerable to psychic and etheric attack.

They're hard to defend because they're behind you and out of reach. When you get hit there etherically, it can feel like a sharp skewer going into your back. Sometimes, if you get a mate to press the points for you, you'll notice how sore they are.

In Teutonic mythology, Siegfried the dragon slayer killed the dragon, and then he bathed in the dragon's blood to make himself immortal and impenetrable to attack. While he bathed, a leaf from a linden tree fell onto his back, so that was the only place on his body that wasn't washed in the dragon's blood. As a result, that was the only spot where Siegfried was vulnerable to attack.

That is why I named the points the "linden points." I found the story of Siegfried's leaf very coincidental. The spots on your back are very real.

On Shape-
Shifting Reptiles

A few years ago, I spent four days talking to author David Icke and his wife in an Irish hotel. He believes that the world is run by shape-shifting humans that are in fact low-level reptiles from another dimension. The fact that our leaders are a bit demonic is obvious to many, but shape-shifting reptiles sounds a bit far-fetched.

Humans carry with them little demons that they incubate and keep warm—you see that all the time. They're usually very active, dark blobs that are located between the navel and the top of the pubic bone or in the center of the chest, but until just recently I'd never seen anyone change into a reptile.

Then I met a lady from South America. She was very well educated and quite imposing in the way she carried herself. What I noticed was that she had very dangerous eyes. Almost everything

hidden about a human is in their eyes or on their lips. Over a period of about two or three minutes, I saw her develop a zigzag spine like a dinosaur's, and then her face elongated to become more snoutlike to reveal reptilian teeth. I was about five yards behind her rear end at the time, but she knew I was watching her going through her shape-shift, and then she turned and smiled. It was the spookiest grin—pure evil—and I'll never forget it.

She's not a politician or even a person with power over others, but the whole reptilian thing became clearer in my mind. Now that I've seen the shape-shift process in real life, I've begun to wonder. There's a lot of hidden stuff in the world.

On Acquiring Knowledge

Metaphysics is knowing that potentially you know everything. It's knowing that you know nothing . . . or very little, anyway. It's knowing that you're happy with that.

On Confidence

Step across the line—believe in yourself. Agree to be right, even when sometimes you might be wrong. In an eternal sense, there's only one category: right. It's all about lessons, isn't it?

On Simplifying
Your Life

Try for a relatively spotless existence. Trust
that all will be okay. Simplicity is the key. The
Living Spirit in all things doesn't have anger.
The Living Spirit doesn't worry about having
to pay the rent. Simplify. Bring up the balance. Make the outer game so simple that it
doesn't impinge or infringe on the inner you.
Keep to the path that has the least resistance.
Allow your inner life to catch up. Simplicity is
the state of becoming nothing again.

On Becoming Precise

To raise your energy and become more, it helps you to learn to make your life precise. Be clear with people. Don't make promises that you don't want to keep. Be punctual. Have little or no unfinished business. Make each step clean and faultless. Focus. Use as little as possible. Disturb nothing or very little. Clean up your life. Tie up loose ends as you move along.

On Serenity

Yin is a composed serenity, a subtle sense of dignity, a delicate belief in self. It's the grace of God in all things. Identify with the yin; it brings you composure, and that helps keep you safe. Nothing should be allowed to destroy that serenity. Serenity comes with softness. It comes through silently observing your life. Touch it. Hold it. Let it shine from your heart.

On Humility

Be humble if you can; arrogance will drag you toward the gates of hell.

On the Sensuality of Life

Abundance is not just money; it's an appreciation for life, its sensuality. It's the love of fine things—like the beauty of a flower, a swim in a cold lake on a hot day, or a plum tree full of fruit. Abundance is a whole gamut of wonderful things: one's friendships, one's relationships, one's experience of life. Many live in prison cells of sensual poverty—they don't open their hearts to the sensuality of life and accept its gifts.

On Life's Banquet

What's the point of being invited to the incredible banquet of life if you're so wrapped up in the neurosis of being at the banquet that you forget to eat?

On Individuality
in Relationships

It's important to understand that whomever you choose to be with is an individual. They can never be you and you can never be them. You should honor that individuality in them, and you should honor yourself. That understanding is sacrosanct. Then the relationship that develops escalates into an incredible crescendo of energy. Entrapment is ugly—allow people the space to be.

On Agreeing
with Everyone

If you want to get to heaven and find peace, you'll have to agree with everyone before you die. The celestial isn't allowed to disagree—it has to love, accept, and forgive everyone, no matter what. Try to make everyone right. Even when they're wrong, forgive them and accept them.

I used to tell people at my seminars, "Think of someone you detest and make them right; imagine hugging them and forgiving them, and at least be neutral toward them." Imagine Hitler standing in front of you. Could you forgive him and love him and make him right? Hard, eh? But the celestial accepts and forgives everyone, and so will you . . . if you want to get to heaven, that is.

It took me 30 years to accept this concept of agreeing. Now I agree with agreeing.

On the Eternal Tao

Become the Tao! Be like nature, big in your feelings. Then you can love everything, because once you become larger than life, you can then incorporate all of it into your heart.

On the Supernatural

There are trillions of beings on Earth in every populated square mile that we can't see. The reason we can't see them is because the oscillation of our brain cells is fast. If you can slow your brain speed to low theta, close to delta (three to four cycles per second), you'll see supernatural beings all around you. Some are very small, like etheric midgets or fleas; others are the size of a human. And then, of course, there are millions of UFOs.

If you look up at any patch of clear blue sky, there are a hundred or more UFOs in the immediate vicinity between you and, say, a distance of five miles. But evil can't touch you unless you have a disdain for humanity or a hidden evil within you.

On UFOs

UFOs intrigue people, as they believe they're from elsewhere in the universe. It's faintly possible, but most of the UFOs we see are local gangsters. They're etheric beings that are part of the Earth plane even though they can shape-shift and fly about. They seek heat to survive. When the world was electrified and mobile phones offered them microwave towers, they expanded over a period of 30 years or so by the trillion. Some are as small as a tennis ball, but they can take on many sizes and shapes: the classic saucer shape, the oil-barrel look, flying triangles, the broom handles and brown blobs, and so on.

Their tactic is to establish mystery and to entice humans to fall into their control. A UFO is an entity, a demonic being that can read your mind. Most of the UFOs are fairly powerless, but there are some that are very strong; they have a pulse that they can hit you with that really hurts. If you don't give yourself to them by seeking them out or approving of them, you don't enable them to come into your energy, so eventually they go away. But they know how to use fear and mystery to entrap you, so you should be careful. And you should keep kids away, as they're also vulnerable to the long-term influence of the UFOs, which is based on evil and control.

Few realize that the UFOs exercise a great influence on our planet, as they can secretly speak to the minds of people enticing them toward the demonic. But in the end, the UFOs will fall from the sky. There's a force here that has just arrived that is intent on bringing them down. First the UFOs will almost completely disappear from the Northern Hemisphere. Then they'll be forced south, toward the equator and South America. Then after a few more years, they'll be beaten out of there as well. They're finished, but not quite yet.

On "Where Is Hell?"

Hell is a feeling; it's a coldness of spirit, but it's also a place. We know from watching the Morph that there's a hell world that the ghouls come up from that is below us. I call it "240 down."

Imagine that you're in the center of a compass and are facing north. Drop your arms by your side; then take your left arm out about a foot from your hip and move it one foot backward behind you, and point.

That is 240 degrees down, because it's 240 degrees around the compass from north, and it's below us at an angle of 45 degrees. It doesn't matter if you twist to face another way—you're always in the center, and all the dimensions twist with you, so the hell world is always 240 degrees below you. All manner of devilish entities come up through the floor from there; that's why you should avoid standing over a drain in the street. It leaves you vulnerable.

On "Where Is Heaven?"

There's a mirror-world beside us at 90 degrees, so if you're facing north, it's beside you (west). Parts of it are heavenly and celestial, and other parts are populated by evil spirits. There's also a celestial world that's above us at a place I call "45 up."

Imagine that you're in the center of a compass and are facing north; raise your right arm up pointing up at an angle of 45 degrees, and without moving your body, point to the right, where northeast would be. That's 45 up, because it's 45 degrees around a compass from north to northeast; and it's at an upward angle of 45 degrees as well. There *is* a celestial world there—very beautiful.

On Nature Spirits

I try to stay away from any discussions on nature spirits, as it leads to dippy ideas of diaphanous beings flitting from flower to flower. It's more correct to think of the spirits of nature as energies, very big ones. There's a secret here that very few people know: The spirits of nature rule this universe. They created it.

Put aside little fairies, and think of spiritual beings quadrillions of years old, much older than our quite-new universe. These beings are massive. They're a body of energy that spreads across trillions of light years. They're conscious entities that exist in a hyperdimensional state as a membrane, like a vast sheet of digital symbols and numbers stretching across eternity, dimensions upon dimensions. Imagine a force of nature that's a dimension of itself—a gift, the way that electricity is a gift. Without it, we wouldn't have stars, because they're born when bolts of electricity hit particles of gas in space.

We little humans and the universe are inside a vast Being, and as I said before, every human has the potential to become a new universe. Our concept of God as a bloke on a throne is a bit limited.

On the Descent of the Goddess

If you read the last entry here on nature spirits, I'd go on to say that the descent of the goddess is a phenomenon of those vast nature spirits. It has already begun; we see it as the fingers of two hands threading between each other. The power of the goddess is a dimension of itself (many dimensions), sliding into this 3-D world between our 3-D molecules. She will transform humanity and our lives on Earth. It is mind flip to see the goddess as a mystical force spread across the universe, rather than a celestial human of the female gender. She's androgynous, you know. Not many realize that; she's not really feminine, but more neutral and eternal.

On Spiritual Growth

In the land of the spiritually blind, the one-eyed man is king, even if he's wearing a contact lens. Any progress is encouraging. We need all the help we can get.

On Deepak Chopra

Deepak was recently on the *Larry King Live* show saying that our society is morally and spiritually bankrupt. He's right in a way. History shows us that just before an empire or society implodes, it becomes self-indulgent and evil. The gaiety and drugs and permissiveness of the 1920s gave way to the restriction of the 1930s, which gave way to the wars of the 1940s, which gave way to rock 'n' roll and the recovery of the 1950s. It's a cycle. Deepak is a gentleman, very polite, so if he tells us we are morally and spiritually bankrupt, we ought to listen.

The Wealth of the Nation

The wealth of the nation is the individual man and woman, the working people of the country. We create the wealth, and the government gets to play with the proceeds. They get to spend your cash pretty much in secret, in any way they like. There's no point in getting pissed off—ignore them. Hopefully, they'll go away.

On Banks

I've never been very keen on banks. It's not polite the way they ask so many personal questions. Plus, they have a way of making you wrong all the time. When you have loads of cash in the bank, they don't thank you; and when you screw up, they pounce on you like you're a Commie and a rat. It's not your fault that you can't count. Let's face it, if you could count, what the hell would you need the bloody bank for?

On Knockin' Yourself Out

If you're knockin' yourself out, struggling like crazy, what you're saying is, "I don't know what I'm doing, and I'm too stupid or idle to change it." Fix the problem quick—stress is the silent killer of our people.

On Organizing
Your Time

The way to control your life is to
control your time. If you don't have
enough time, it says that you're a bit
out of control. Analyze what's important in your life—keep the best and
bag the rest.

On Fluidity

Many people are overweight in things. And whereas at the beginning, things gave you pleasure, in the end they don't really matter anymore. They drain you because you have to look after them. You've got to service them, protect them, insure them, and polish them. That's why I dislike cars: You have to look after the bloody things. Someone famous once said, "The things you own wind up owning you." He or she was right.

On Achieving
Your Goals

Genghis Khan started with a tribe of 17 people, including his mother. He conquered everything. It seems to me that you don't need much in life other than enthusiasm and your mum.

On Winners

Losers bother me. Sorry, that's probably not very nice. I try to have compassion for them, but my compassion is a bit watery thin. Except for rare occasions, stay away from losers—they're not a good affirmation for who you are. You can slip away without making them wrong.

On Developing Plans

The fact is that there are all sorts of ways of doing all sorts of things. If you get too involved in what other people say can and can't be done, you tend to lose the focus of your plan. Work on your plan silently without discussing it with others, except when you have to.

On Confusion

If you've ever been confused, I can fix it for you in one minute flat. But you have to agree to follow my instructions to the letter. You get rid of confusion by agreeing to never ask any questions. You can't be confused unless you ask questions—don't ask; just accept things.

On Natural Love

If we could reach the point within our minds where we had few, or perhaps no, thoughts at all, then the natural love and goodness that comes up from our hearts, the connection we have with all things, would spring forth and we would enter a state of perpetual joy. Thinking leads to irritation and sadness.

On the Reflection of Marriage

In marriage or in any relationship, you have to learn to communicate. What's fun about relationships is that the other person reflects back to you who you are. When you're married, your spouse tends to let you know your shortcomings extremely quickly, like in about two minutes flat! So you learn about yourself and begin to see yourself in a new light.

On Young Children

The way to help children is to allow them to be who they are. I think people are beginning to understand that children are grown-up spirits in little bodies. It's also important to remember that the child's spirit (its Higher Self) has a certain characteristic that will gradually draw him or her into various experiences in life that will materialize either in the positive or the negative depending on the individual's focus.

There's nothing much you can do about the eventual direction children will take. All you can do is offer the best tools possible for handling life, and applaud when they do well and be there when they fall on their faces.

On Going to School

My lad and his little mates would run around the house till the early hours, and then they'd always be reluctant to go to school the next day. I found it such a struggle trying to get them to do what I wanted—endless aggravation.

So I called a board meeting in the kitchen for all the little bandits, and I told them that they could go to school or not as they wished; I wasn't going to fight anymore. And I wasn't going to tell them to eat or not eat. They could organize themselves and eat what they wanted whenever they wanted it. I had a cook at that time, so that helped me a lot.

For the first few days, it was mayhem, but on day four, I woke up to see all the little guys lined up dressed and clean and ready for school. I was shocked. They told me they had a test that day, and they felt the need to be responsible and show up. Once I stopped trying to impose my will, they went to bed more or less in good time, and they looked after each other and all went to school like good little tykes. I never had a problem after that. It was pure bliss.

On the
Naturalness of Kids

You learn a lot from kids—they're so natural. It's amazing that we grown-ups forget so quickly how easy naturalness is. Let's face it—it wasn't that many years ago that we stood with a group of people in the drawing room and we peed on the carpet without so much of an "If you please" or "Do you mind."

On Coffee Shops

At a coffee shop in Vancouver, I saw a sign that said: "Children left unattended will be sold as sandwiches." Funny.

On Family Life

One of the things I like about family life is that you get to bitch and argue with people whom you know and love . . . in the comfort of your own home.

On Chance

It is said that you should never leave anything to chance. But in operating like that, chance never leaves anything to you.

On Overworking

For years I was a workaholic. Then one day I changed my mind. I realized how I used overworking as a way of avoiding fear; I used it as a death-avoidance mechanism. If I worked like crazy, I would forget to be scared. Overworking for long periods of time is dangerous to your health. Now I'm self-unemployed. I like it better that way.

On Financial Enlightenment

Sooner or later, people realize that in order to be free, you have to have money—sad but true. If you don't concentrate on money, you'll never have any. And if you don't have any, it's difficult to be truly free. I'm not saying that you can't join a Buddhist monastery someplace and just have your little grain of rice each day, and then ol' Zendo Bendo comes along and thwacks you over the ear with a stick and you touch nirvana. That's one way. But somehow I think my way is more pleasing.

On the Concrete Overcoat

A person who isn't aware, who resists opening up to new perceptions, walks in a concrete overcoat. It's hard to operate through life like that. You have to be open to change and new ideas, even if that's a little threatening at first—and even if it means that something or someone will come along and turn all of your sacred cows into dog meat.

On the Arrogance of Ignorance

The arrogance of ignorance has always bothered me. Often the less people know, the more insistent they are. So many don't have a clue as to what's happening in the world, or why. There's something terribly scary about that, especially when they wind up in positions of power.

On Personal Enlightenment

Falling in love with yourself—not in an egocentric sense—but falling in love because you've forgiven yourself, you appreciate yourself, and you're at peace with yourself, is a wonderful thing. Knowing that you're this carefree scamp allows you to fall in love with life; and you can see laughter, stillness, and beauty in all things. You can see the courage that's naturally in your heart. And you can watch that courage walk out into life and demonstrate your mastery over it. Gradually, that mastery will grant you enlightenment.

On Emotional Discipline

Emotional discipline is not the act of not having emotions. It's more a matter of not allowing them to run amok all over your life without your taking a look at them. "Hey, why am I upset?" "Why am I angry?" Stuff like that. Emotions are okay as long as you don't inflict them on others; that can be evil and/or manipulative. Try to be aware and to share your emotional feelings without making others wrong in the process.

On Overstimulation

The problem with the constant stimulation of modern life is that you gradually become numb to it, and you have to create more and more stimulation in order for it to have any effect. Sooner or later we find that we're cramming our day full of stuff in order to get over the anguish we feel because the day is crammed full of stuff. Weird, eh?

On Disadvantages

There was a young man once who had been born with a defect. One of his legs was much shorter than the other. His lack of mobility bothered him greatly. So he climbed up a mountain to visit a great sage who was reputed to live high in the valleys. He literally crawled and pulled himself high up that mountain for days until he finally came upon the sage. He asked, "Sir, I was born with this defect, and one of my legs is much shorter than the other. What should I do?"

The sage paused in silence for a moment and then said, "Limp." The young man understood. He went off and became a great healer.

On Abandonment

If you were abandoned emotionally as a child, you'll find it hard to trust people. If your father ran away, you may be suspicious of men. If your mother died or she floated out of the family early, your attitude toward women may be slightly warped.

Abandonment gives rise to addictions. Adults who were abandoned in childhood feel an emptiness within that they may try to medicate or appease with drugs or alcohol, or sometimes they develop an addiction to pornography and sex. These pople are quick to get angry about very small things, and they see betrayal at every turn.

The trick is to visualize yourself at the age when you got hurt and then mentally pick up that small child and hold him or her to your chest and say, "I'm your Daddy or Mummy now; you are safe. I'll look after you in this lifetime." It's cute and it works.

If you don't treat the psychology of the wounded child, it's hard to cure addiction.

On Traveling

I've traveled constantly in my life. Wander-lust must have been in my veins at birth. I find that I use places up, and maybe you're the same. When you first go to a place, it seems magical and interesting, and every-thing is new and fresh and it exhilarates you. Then one morning you wake up and the cute little store on the corner is not so cute, and a cockroach walks across your plate at the little bistro you so loved. All the people you see tell you all the things they told you last week, and suddenly you realize that you've drained the place of the magic it held for you.

At that point, my mind begins a faint hum. It's unintelligible at first, but as I lis-ten carefully, I can hear it getting louder and louder; and I realize that it's saying to me, "Airport! Airport! Airport!"

On Wanderlust

I've never been able to settle; I've been to 58 countries. I travel for eight months of each year. A little wanderlust is wonderful, but 30 years of wanderlust is a bit more suspect. I go home for a few months and then I think, *I wonder what Guatemala is like?* So off I trot. Then I think, *Well, the music is nice in Cuba,* and so on. I've got a suitcase and a little computer and an old pair of shoes . . . and not much else.

Through the trance state, I started to see myself in another dimension, a mirror-world, so I did wanderlust in there for five years. Now I do wanderlust in two places, the outer world and the inner one. I forgive myself, saying, "It's all divine madness."

On Letting Go

Often, in order to properly discover yourself, you have to be prepared to let go. That can make you a bit insecure. It's as if you're forced to lose yourself and many of those facets of your personality that you hold so dear in order for you to quiet the mind and return gradually back to the source, whereupon you discover yourself again—the "real" you, not the trapped, fake one.

On Perfection

None of us came to the physical plane to be perfect. It's an important fact. Being imperfect makes this spiritual quest so bloody marvelous. Imperfection allows you to develop forgiveness in your heart—not only forgiveness of self, but a forgiveness that you offer others. You can cut them a little slack, Jack. You don't have to push people to be perfect. And as you grant that forgiveness to yourself, then others, in turn, grant you more leeway; and soon you begin to see how beautifully bizarre life is.

On Controlling People Through Lending

Debt is how the status quo controls the world. You can have all the rules and regulations you want, and you can build massive police forces and tax systems, but debt is the easiest way of controlling the population; and those who have power over us know that. That's why they make debt so easy to assume. When the Western world gave up its empires, all it did was lend the lesser-developed countries plenty of money and "Hey, presto!" all the control mechanisms were still there.

Don't get suckered in. If you're in debt, work on a plan to get out. Being debt free is the common man's way of saying "Up yours" to the system.

On Personal Debt

In attempting to materialize our hopes and dreams, we often commit to great amounts of personal debt. What I found was that I used debt as a stopgap. It's easier to borrow a bunch of money than to think of ways of materializing projects with what one has at hand, or by borrowing a lot less. It seemed to me that I used debt instead of creative cleverness. Also, it was my impatience that wanted to borrow money. But debt made me sad; I hated being trapped by the commitment.

One day I banned myself from all debt. It took me three years to pay everything off, but by forcing myself to operate on a cash basis, I stimulated my financial prowess; and everything came together stronger and more solid than ever before. I sold stuff and spent less.

The end result was that in a thousand days or so, I turned several hundred thousand dollars of debt into that exact amount in cash assets. I never looked back, and I never took on any more debt. It was 24 years ago when I dropped debt off at the great bus stop of life.

On Lips

Lips are handy; they stop your mouth from fraying. You can learn a lot about people by looking at their lips. It's as if the central statement of a person's life is gradually etched on their lips, thereby changing their shape to accommodate whatever is being said. Rabbits have nice noses and nice lips.

On the Tooth Fairy

I always believed in the tooth fairy—up until I was seven or eight, anyway. Then I got rattled, wondering what the hell the fairy did with all those second-hand teeth.

On Men in
Brown Polyester Suits

Beware of men in brown polyester suits. They'll either try to hug you at the church door or they'll try to sell you something.

On Negativity

If through insecurity you concentrate on misfortune, that act of concentration draws to you the very things you've been hoping to avoid. It comes along and bites you on the bum. It finds you. In fact, it will cross town to get you.

On Learning
Through Mistakes

We came to the Earth plane without a manual. We just plopped in here, and we have to muddle along trying to understand what the hell's going on without anyone really showing us. If you allow the guilt trips of life to mess with you, it will rot your brain. You needed the mistakes you made. And the people you impacted through those mistakes needed you. And so, bit by bit, realizing that, you can come to a healing of your life.

On Regimen

There's a big difference between regimen and discipline. Regimen is a system for the simple-minded drone. You might need discipline, but if you're a carefree scamp, why would you need regimen?

On Sexuality

Sexuality can sometimes make people nervous. It's always too much, too little, too this, and too that. Sex is somehow connected to the number 2. That's all the numerology I know.

On the Illogical

Beyond logic and facts and all of our accumulated scientific knowledge, there's the power of spirit, which is often illogical. Things happen that are wonderful and unexpected and that come from nowhere; it's pointless to try to work them out. Each event is a manifestation of your energy—the outward expressions of your feelings that you get to experience and enjoy. It's the energy of spirit responding to what you are and what you've become. Who needs logic to be a part of that? You just need energy.

On Accepting Responsibility

Once you accept that the world is basically beautiful and that you are 100 percent responsible for your evolution, you understand that if something jumps out of the sidewalk and bites you on the bum, it's a manifestation of your energy. You also understand that life is a teaching symbol of the quality of the inner you. So if you need to know, "How am I doing?" look around you. Every second of every moment of the day, the Great Spirit is giving you a printout of how things are going.

On Seeking
Recognition

As your energy grows and you work on your-self, people will be pulled to you, and you'll wind up helping them. There's a point on the journey where one tends to seek some kind of recognition from the inner light for the work one has done.

But you'll be disappointed to discover that the inner dimensions are devoid of thanks and recognition. In the early days, that used to bug me. Then I realized that it's only one's ego that needs the recognition and thanks, and that the part of you that actually did the work—spirit—doesn't need to thank itself.

On Chasing Money

We have to have money, but it's wrong to chase it. In chasing after it, you tend to push it away. Sometimes money is like a skittish girlfriend who's constantly trying to tow you around by the nose, dancing with all the other blokes. The more you chase her, the more she drives you nuts. But sit in the corner and jangle the car keys and she'll come home with you . . . because she's not up for walking, and deep down she likes you.

On Money, Emotion, and Security

To the man in the street, money is like God. It gives him permission to act and become special, and through it he experiences a sense of security. It grants him the ability to be important. Because it's such a symbol of status and security, it's natural that money and emotion go hand in hand. That's why everybody is tearing around like chickens with their heads cut off trying to get it.

However, the more you surround your moneymaking ventures with emotion and insecurity, the less money you'll have. That explains why most people don't have any real money to speak of, in spite of going bonkers 15 hours a day for years, trying to acquire it. Once you "click" your mind from "Money equals security," to "Money equals creative freedom," then you relax and you don't have to chase it. It will just jump in your lap. You'll like that a lot better.

On the Psychology of Selling

Money is so inexorably linked to security in the mind of the common man. It's vitally important to remember that when you're trying to sell him something. In order for him to transfer his money to you, he has to feel safe. The easiest way to make him feel safe is to subjugate your ego, get underneath him psychologically, and really act out of love and support. You have to take the buyer past whatever survival considerations he might have. You do this by clearly defining the benefit of the item or service you're selling, by reassuring him that he's safe and that the world is okay and that things will last forever.

That's what he wants to hear. So tell him that. If you both believe it, it will help make that a reality. Why not?

On Agreeing to Be Rich

Once you feel good about yourself, all of a sudden money flows, and all you're looking to do is to go beyond the emotion surrounding money and open the faucet. The wealth of the world is so fantastic that if you divided it up among the people equally, everyone would be a millionaire. So our natural state is to be millionaires. Anything less is either where you've found yourself by birth or where you've put yourself through time. Poverty in the Western world is unnatural. Once you agree that your natural state is to be rich, wealth starts to find you. Change your mind. Let's go shopping!

On Creativity

Creativity is one of the greatest expressions of the God-Force on the physical plane. It's a test to go past the awkwardness we feel in creating things and to create them anyway. It's fine to create things for your own pleasure, but the quintessence of creativity is doing something that you love to do and getting paid for it. How much more brilliant can it get? It's not work, is it?

The problem arises when you have to present your creativity to the marketplace and face the possibility of rejection. Fear sets in, and the mind can suck you into all sorts of ego-oriented opinions that keep you poor. I feel that much of the snobbery surrounding art is a by-product of the artist's ego and fear. Rather than creating something that people will buy, the artist waxes lyrical about not wanting to besmirch the purity of his or her art by adjusting to commercial reality. But the reality is that if the public won't buy a cow turd nailed to a canvas, it's not their fault. The fault lies in the artist's mediocrity or in his or her lack of perception, not the taste of the buying public. So if you have to adjust somewhat to make it work, I suggest that you compromise and pay the rent.

On Negative Yearning

Don't yearn for things that you don't have. The emotion of yearning creates a powerful negative affirmation that pushes the things you desire away from you. Why is that? Because through negative yearning, you devalue the power of the present—that which is real right now. Then your ability to materialize your dreams is lessened because your current energy is lowered by your negativity. If you want a Porsche, don't pine. Say to yourself, "I want that car. I know I can have it, for in my heart I feel that it's already a part of my life. Meanwhile, I'm driving this ol' banger 'cause it feels like a Porsche to me."

On Staying Balanced

In America it costs you $750 just to walk through the door of a hospital, so you're forced to stay balanced and care for yourself. Your whole body says, "Forget it, we can't afford to get sick." Then if you look at other countries that have socialized free medicine like the British National Health System, you can see how ill health is a way of life there. If your body conks out, you just haul it around to the government and they'll fix it for free. There's no incentive to stay balanced and to choose a healthy way of life. Free medicine seems to make people less healthy.

On Being
Self-Motivated

Self-motivation goes back to intent, courage, determination, and finally the sense of an "I am what I am" sort of acceptance. In our society, we don't teach our children the ways of the ancient warrior-sages. We teach them to become dependent and helpless. Our vapid, sometimes bland societies are built on junk food, television, and titillation because people don't grant empowerment to themselves. There's no charismatic spirit to sustain them.

The immediacy of metaphysical reality is what grants one excitement. Animals stay extremely in tune with their surroundings because they're both the hunter and the hunted. In Western civilized democracies, we're so comfortable, closeted, and coddled. There's a safety net that makes everything guaranteed and safe. If you fall below a certain level, the great paramedic in the sky comes and gives you food stamps or something. If we cut all that out and there was a psychic immediacy to survival, then everybody would get charismatically involved. You can see this confirmed in history. A country like England needs a war every so often just to keep its adrenals going.

On Collecting
Experiences

The spiritual warrior understands that to go beyond the Earth plane, he or she will have to collect experiences. By experiencing life, you become familiar with it; by becoming familiar with it, you go beyond fear.

On Transcending Fear

I used to teach seminars on facing fear, so naturally I've thought a lot about how we as humans transcend this emotion. The conclusion I came to was that we can't completely eliminate fear, for we can never know everything. So the name of the game is to transmute fear from a paralyzing force into a motivating force, rather than wasting time trying to suppress it or transcend it.

A small percentage of your fears are real, and they should be respected; they're valuable. They keep you safe and motivate you into action. But the majority of your fears just constitute negative dialogue that dribbles from the mind. The way to work with that is to begin to talk to the fear as if it were another person. So you say, "Thank you, I appreciate that possibility you've just offered me. However, given the current circumstances of my life, I don't accept that negative possibility as a reality in my life. Furthermore, the idea of my being eaten by a wild animal here at the bus station is a little remote. But thank you anyway, and ciao, baby."

On Hope and Courage

If you believe and trust in the Great Spirit, it sustains you. You may not understand how it operates in your life, but it's there, all will come to pass, and there will be balance in the end. So you should never give up hope. Even if you can't see how things will turn out, just continue to know and believe that the Force is with you and that the outcome will be the best possible, given the circumstances.

Tenacity allows you to hold on long enough for the Universe to deliver a solution to you. You concentrate on the major things and allow the God-Force to figure out the details. Courage, dear friend, courage. Once you feel that you're truly a part of the God-Force, nothing is ever lost, for God cannot lose itself. All negativity is transmuted to goodness and light in the end.

On Eternal Love

In the eternity of things, love isn't really an emotion. It is respecting others—allowing them to be whatever they wish to be, even if what they are might seem evil. The greatest love you can express is not to judge others, but to surrender and allow them time to come to correct solutions on their own. For within our humanity there's a long-forgotten dream, one in which we remember our true heritage in the abode of light, and where we are truly infinite.

On Why Eternity Has No Future

Here's something quirky. It won't help you much, but it's really interesting. I discovered during my travels in the inner worlds that eternity has no future. One imagines that eternity stretches into the future forever, so it sounds like a contradiction.

Here's the explanation: Anything moving at less than the speed of light can't be eternal; it has to be finite, so it does have a future, albeit a future that will eventually end. If something like an undiscovered, hypothetical particle were moving faster than the speed of light, it would be going backward in time, not forward. So it would not have a future, only a past that it would be traveling toward.

If it were possible to move exactly at the speed of light, you would experience an eternal now, but not a future. Quirky stuff. I have a feeling that what we call time is all an illusion.

On Gay People

I've never quite understood why society discriminates against gay men and women. Why should a person's sexual preference be of any concern to others? If a gay couple treats each other with kindness and respect and they love each other, that surely must add to the goodness in the world.

Love is love, whether it's mother and child, female with female, or friend with friend. You can't stick love and its physical expression, sex, into a little box and say that we'll only approve of love if and when it's expressed under circumstances that we consider acceptable. In a world where there's so much ugly energy, any expression of love should be encouraged and applauded.

On
Dysfunctional
People

If you try to hold up a weak person, you're often endorsing their dysfunction. If, God forbid, you decide that you don't want to hold them up anymore, it can cause anger and retribution. There's a subtle balance between compassion and enabling people to be dysfunctional and unwell. It's a tough one; I've been bitten loads of times backing people who turned out to be dishonest or hopeless. I go more carefully now.

On Stress Control

There are all sorts of handy techniques offered nowadays to busy executives to help them manage stress in their lives. Here's my technique: Retire early . . . like yesterday.

On New Age Philosophies

One of the criticisms of the New Age is that it created dippy people of the "soggy-Kleenex" variety, people just as weak as those left behind. Yet the New Age offered an alternative spirituality based on naturalness, truth, and an unpretentious lifestyle. I'm a great believer in alternative medicine, and the New Age movement did great work in bringing alternative healing into the mainstream. All in all, I think the New Age movement deserves a pat on the back, as it has helped people enormously.

On Ungluing

The world is sort of ungluing. The emotional base of people is weaker now. Many are hypnotized by glitter that is outside of them. The building is burning, and they just keep turning the music up louder so the roar of the flames can't be heard. The sensible ones are taking note of conditions, and walking slowly to the fire escape before it's too late.

On Society and Drugs

The reason why society doesn't like drugs is partly because the dopers remind us of all our dysfunctions and the stuff we're hooked on. It's a shadow thing. Middle-class people who are stoned out of their heads on legal drugs point the finger at working-class drug users. People in the U.S. consume 70 million Valium tablets every day. Add to that all the other tranquilizers, uppers, downers, and booze, and what we have is a society that's mostly slightly stoned all of the time.

If you want to fix the drug problem, you're going to have to fix society first. Second, you're going to have to wean everyone off their addictions. I'm glad that's not my job.

On Busy Work

If you analyze your life, you'll probably find that much of the effort you put in gets you little or no return. The mind creates "busy work," which is nothing more than rushing around without a definite plan or direction, killing time until the day ends. By identifying which of your actions bring rewards and which do not, you eliminate the dross and make way for simplicity and success.

Ideally, your life should be designed so that your needs come to *you,* rather than you having to chase after them. By being organized and disciplined, you'll tend to hit the bull's-eye with just one dart. That leaves you time to eat chocolate and go fishing!

On Minorities
and the Impartiality
of the God-Force

The disadvantage faced by minorities in society is very real. Yet the God-Force is all about energy, and that divine energy doesn't have any judgment or opinions about people. So anybody can make it if they'll just stop moaning and put in a little effort. As you pull out of the emotion that says, "I am so disadvantaged, ain't that awful," and you concentrate instead on "making it" in life, things improve. I think people are beginning to understand that.

On Living
Your Destiny

You live your own destiny. Nothing should force you or manipulate you or make you be something else. The God-Force doesn't ask you to suffer or struggle or be poor. The God-Force expects you to eventually become free.

On People's Lack

The reason why most people are poorly paid is that they have few skills, and they put little true effort into their labor. If you want abundance, start right now by agreeing that you'll pump energy into your work, as much as it takes for as long as it takes.

Most put the cart before the horse, saying, "Give me a pay raise and I'll work harder." First you put the energy in, then you crank up your pay demands. If you go at it the other way, you may get little raises, but you won't get major leaps to new levels. If you want to get a pay raise in 30 days, you should dress immaculately, get in half an hour early, leave late, work really hard, and offer to do extra things for the boss even if he or she wants you to walk their pet poodle. After 30 days, go in and ask for a pay raise because you worked hard and deserve it, and if you get a flat "No!" then start looking around for another job, because your boss obviously doesn't appreciate your efforts, but others will.

On Making
Life Sacred

How does something become sacred? It becomes sacred by people saying, "This is sacred." There's no other way. So St. Matilda's toenail in a box is just that, until someone says, "This relic is holy and special." So how do you make your life sacred? You say, "This is sacred," and you treat it that way. By making your life special, others begin to treat you differently.

On Falling in Love

When we fall in love, what attracts us most about other people is how different they are from us. Look at all the little short guys who marry Amazonian ladies, or the princesses who marry their chauffeurs. Once hitched, we tend to change ourselves to accommodate what we think our partner wants of us, then we try to change them to suit our view of life. So, what starts out as an exciting relationship full of spontaneity and contrast becomes a life of strict rules, making everything seem the same. We wind up dancing to each other's tune.

It's so simple to criticize our mate, for we are close to this position, and we know so much about his or her weaknesses. But in doing so, what we're really saying is that we're not comfortable with ourselves. It's almost impossible to go beyond a weakness by concentrating on it. For by concentrating on it, you energize it. It's better for both of you to develop and enhance your strengths.

Many women pick weak spouses, and in doing so, they sentence themselves to a lifetime of struggle. They put out, "Send me a wet blanket," and sooner or later they pull to themselves a real idiot. "I'm getting married," they say, and their Mum replies, "That's nice, dear, who's the guy?" "Luke." "Luke who?" "Luke Warm. We'll struggle like crazy and have lots of lukewarm kids."

On the Discipline of the Tao

There's no book you can study to learn the Tao, because if you read about it in a book, it isn't the Tao. I read the Tao Te Ching and realized I wasn't any the wiser. So to discover the Tao, I went out into nature. Every day for three years I woke at 4:30 A.M. and walked in the forest in the dark. By doing so, my mind became centered, even though at the beginning I was a bit freaked out. But by doing the discipline of walking, I got a perception of energy. I began to understand what the Tao is. The Taoists revere nature because they say that it's a pure manifestation of the God-Force, uncluttered by emotion or limitation. I finally got it . . . well, bits of it.

On Perception

Perception demands that your mind take note of everything. Walk into a room and force your attention to watch everything, to count everything, to be aware of what is there and what is not there. Doing so as a mental discipline heightens your overall perception of life.

On
Self-Empowerment

Fear keeps you awake and aware. It's an ally. Treat it with respect. Courage is not absence of fear—courage is recognizing fear and operating in spite of it. Fear is an ally that empowers us. Ask yourself, what's the worst thing that can happen?

On Positive
Expectation

Expect the best. Put your mind, your emotions, and your enthusiasm behind that affirmation. Create yourself in an image that's
strong. Where is your mind? See yourself on
the other side—having what it is you want.
Your intention gets you across the line. Focus
your attention, be up for it, and allow the
experience to carry you. Be involved with
your inner self. Know how you feel—be emotionally aware and commit.

On Hiring
or Associating
with People

Once you become more powerful, you'll want to ensure that the people around you are of the same energy. Create a narrow entrance into your life. Get a new team of people. Execute the old order. Create a new empire. Be shrewd. Keep it clean. Put in a few hurdles so that the wimps can't make it into your encampment. That way you and the people around you remain dedicated and strong. It only takes one whiner or a little bad energy to pollute your whole life.

On Being Crafty, Not Sneaky

Craftiness isn't being sneaky. It's just mastering the craft of humanhood. It's easy to operate in the marketplace of life with shrewdness and still be honorable. Craftiness allows you to maximize your benefits with a minimum of effort. Position yourself on the high ground. Use the information that's available to you. Use it to cut corners. That's the craft.

It's not dishonesty, just a shortcut.

On Becoming More Shrewd

Be shrewd. Don't rush to say yes or no. Play the waiting game—control the time frame. When others try to rush you, play dumb. Stall for time. When they try to confront you, engage them by drawing them out of their ego's castle. Get them to show you how brilliant they are. Stimulate their importance. By doing so, they'll lean toward you. In leaning, they lose balance. Then tap them psychologically or emotionally, and before they realize what's happened, they're in open ground with their knickers around their ankles, looking silly.

On Self-Acceptance

Strugglers crave acceptance; they have low self-esteem. This causes them to constantly seek the acceptance and approval of others. Yet, the acknowledgment they seek is rarely forthcoming, and it's usually dissatisfying even when they get it. This causes frustration. By lacking identity—a sense of knowing and accepting who they are—they shift their attention from what is real (inside of them) to the materialistic symbols of life, which aren't real (outside of them). Self-acceptance is the act of turning inward.

On "I Am What I Am"

You've become satisfied with what you have and what you are right now. You have to be happy with your lot in life. Things can be changed, but there are lessons to learn here and now. If those lessons aren't learned, and if you don't accept what you've created for yourself, your energy doesn't move forward. By resisting, and sometimes becoming angry, you stagnate. Today is part of your life's curriculum. Learn it, and tomorrow will look after itself.

On Opinions

That which is struggle to one person is just gentle effort to another. Struggle is always how you feel about something—your opinion and your reaction to the circumstance, not the circumstance itself. To dump struggle, you should get used to asking yourself in each circumstance: "What is my underlying emotion or opinion here?"

On Being Jesus

I met a man who was convinced that he was Jesus. So I knelt down and I asked him for his blessing. What else was I supposed to do? I'm not a psychiatrist, you know.

On Flow

If things don't flow, ask yourself, "Am I going too fast?" or "Am I too slow? Is this the right time?" Usually things take longer than we expect. This is because we can think faster than we can act. So, ideas have to incubate and come together, especially when you need others to help you materialize your dreams. To make life work, you have to face it full frontal, head out with a good plan, and trust in the Great Spirit to deliver. But go toward your goal even if it seems to be a long way off. Nothing will carry you. You will usually have to carry yourself.

On Your Life and the Cast of Characters

To go beyond struggle, you first have to be able to accept the help of others; and second, you have to choose your characters carefully. If you find yourself in a campaign with the cast already set, you must become a crafty "general" and get the most out of your people, given the circumstances, goals, and what the budget allows. Never be afraid to let people go if they're not right.

On "Change Is Natural"

Affirmation: *Change is natural for me. Within it, I experience new and exciting aspects of myself.*

On Karmic Law

A person who violates the rights of others and infringes on their creative freedom creates an energy of restriction around himself. That, in turn, pulls to him others who will violate his rights. It is not "crime and punishment" in the sense of retribution for sin; it is more energy in motion—its consequences, if you like.

On Karma, Day to Day

Most karma is immediate; things happen as a result of balance and imbalance. You're angry today, so you fall off the sidewalk and twist your ankle. You get small warnings. The trick is to become balanced quickly before the energy deteriorates any further.

On Nutritional Discipline

There's no faster way of raising your energy than by adopting good eating habits. The body's nutritional needs become clear, and you gradually become your own healer. You begin to know what you need. The healing process cannot occur unless you maintain an alkaline balance in the foods you eat. There are loads of acid-alkaline food charts on the Internet.

On Discipline in General

Discipline is good for you—it helps you control your life. But too much of the same discipline eventually spins you into the laws of diminishing returns. If you follow the same discipline for years and years, eventually it has no more power for you, and it will become an energy drag rather than an energy booster. Personal discipline is like a muscle. You need to squeeze it, then let it go, then squeeze it some more to keep your disciplines fresh. Change them often, and also have periods of no discipline at all. That will give you the best results.

On War

War is a drag, but it's part of the human psyche to be warlike. We should recognize that and treat it as a disease like drug addiction. If I were secretary-general of the United Nations, I'd set aside a bit of land like the Gobi Desert, and I'd make everyone go and have their battles on that spot. I'd sell tickets and hot dogs and make it into an event. And I'd limit the war to three days. An international committee would declare the winner. We could have medal ceremonies and national anthems, and Nike or Adidas could endorse the boots, and so on. It's not fair when they have wars downtown; it messes with the traffic.

On World Peace

So much of life is just a matter of how you look at things—what your opinion is. Think about world peace. Right now, everybody's trotting about waxing lyrical about how we've gotta have world peace. And a lot of people are all upset and in anguish about the whole thing. If there's 6 billion people in the world and there's approximately 5 million at war, that leaves 5,995 million people who aren't at war today. Perhaps we've got a bit of world peace without even realizing it.

On the Destiny
of the World

I firmly believe that the world
will sort itself out in the end.
Believe it with me. We need all
the supporters we can get!

Author and lecturer **Stuart Wilde** is an urban mystic, a modern visionary; he's written 17 books on consciousness and awareness, including the very successful Taos Quintet, which are considered classics in their genre. They are: *Miracles, Affirmations, The Force, The Quickening,* and *The Trick to Money Is Having Some!.*

Stuart's perceptive and quirky way of writing has won him a loyal readership over the years. He has a simple way of explaining things that hitherto have seemed a mystery. His books have been translated into 15 languages.

Please visit his Websites: **www.stuartwilde.com** and **www.redeemersclub.com**.

NOTES

NOTES

NOTES

NOTES

NOTES

NOTES

NOTES

NOTES

Hay House Titles of Related Interest

Everyday Positive Thinking,
by Louise L. Hay and Friends

Everyday Wisdom, by Dr. Wayne W. Dyer

Never Mind Success . . . Go for Greatness!
by Tavis Smiley

101 Ways to Jump-Start Your Intuition,
by John Holland

Power Thoughts, by Louise L. Hay

Staying on the Path, by Dr. Wayne W. Dyer

———

All of the above are available at your local
bookstore, or may be ordered by visiting:

Hay House USA: **www.hayhouse.com**®
Hay House Australia: **www.hayhouse.com.au**
Hay House UK: **www.hayhouse.co.uk**
Hay House South Africa: **orders@psdprom.co.za**
Hay House India: **www.hayhouseindia.co.in**

———

We hope you enjoyed this Hay House Lifestyles book. If you'd like to receive a free catalog featuring additional Hay House books and products, or if you'd like information about the Hay Foundation, please contact:

Hay House, Inc.
P.O. Box 5100
Carlsbad, CA 92018-5100

(760) 431-7695 or **(800) 654-5126**
(760) 431-6948 (fax) or **(800) 650-5115 (fax)**
www.hayhouse.com® • www.hayfoundation.org

Published and distributed in Australia by: Hay House Australia Pty. Ltd., 18/36 Ralph St., Alexandria NSW 2015 • *Phone:* 612-9669-4299 *Fax:* 612-9669-4144 • www.hayhouse.com.au

Published and distributed in the United Kingdom by: Hay House UK, Ltd., 292B Kensal Rd., London W10 5BE • *Phone:* 44-20-8962-1230 *Fax:* 44-20-8962-1239 • www.hayhouse.co.uk

Published and distributed in the Republic of South Africa by: Hay House SA (Pty), Ltd., P.O. Box 990, Witkoppen 2068 *Phone/Fax:* 27-11-706-6612 • orders@psdprom.co.za

Published in India by: Hay House Publishers India, Muskaan Complex, Plot No. 3, B-2, Vasant Kunj, New Delhi 110 070 *Phone:* 91-11-4176-1620 • *Fax:* 91-11-4176-1630 www.hayhouseindia.co.in

Distributed in Canada by: Raincoast, 9050 Shaughnessy St., Vancouver, B.C. V6P 6E5 • *Phone:* (604) 323-7100 • *Fax:* (604) 323-2600 www.raincoast.com

---

Tune in to **HayHouseRadio.com®** for the best in inspirational talk radio featuring top Hay House authors! And, sign up via the Hay House USA Website to receive the Hay House online newsletter and stay informed about what's going on with your favorite authors. You'll receive bimonthly announcements about Discounts and Offers, Special Events, Product Highlights, Free Excerpts, Giveaways, and more!
www.hayhouse.com®